# Courtroom DNA Testing: A Massive Fraud by the Justice System

## Exposé of Facts

F. Finch

Cadmus Publishing
www.cadmuspublishing.com

Copyright © 2023 F. Finch

Published by Cadmus Publishing
www.cadmuspublishing.com
Port Angeles, WA

ISBN: 978-1-63751-389-7

All rights reserved. Copyright under Berne Copyright Convention, Universal Copyright Convention, and Pan-American Copyright Convention. No part of this book may be reproduced, stored in a retrieval system, or transmitted in any form, or by any means, electronic, mechanical, photocopying, recording or otherwise, without prior permission of the author.

# Courtroom "DNA" Testing
## PCR STR LCN

1. Firstly, it must be understood that there are many different types of testing. However, forensic DNA testing should not be confused with the medical genomic linear sequencing, gene editing or cloning technologies used in the medical field.

2. In short, the initial methods used to gain admissibility were, in part, a "direct analysis of genomic DNA" and others utilized (PCR) polymerase chain reaction, such as the D1S80 test; a hybrid method. "Manufactured evidence."

3. Forensic DNA testing was admitted into evidence virtually unchallenged; and the first three appellate decisions in this country, "The defendants had no defense experts;" Andrew v. State, 533 So. 2d. 841 (Fla app 1988); Coby v. State, 80 Md. App 559A 2d 391 (1989); Spencer v. Commonwealth, 238 VA 275 SE 2d 775 (1989).

4. As an initial note, lawyers must rely on experts and it is not the expert's responsibility to train lawyers on their discipline. "It is the lawyer's responsibility for the responsible practice of law to educate themselves on the methods of forensic practices," and to know what acceptable legal methods are employed, and if they are even recognized by the scientific community; what problems have been experienced, and what if any corrective measures have been taken and, "Not blindly accept conclusions by experts who have 'vested interests' in the technology."

5. (RFLP) Restriction Fragment Length Polymorphism (VNTR) Variable Number Tandem Repeats, among others, remained the gold standard of forensic DNA testing until another method was introduced, PCR-STR, Polymerase Chain Reaction/ Short Tandem Repeat.

6. In 1992 the National Research Counsel whose members are drawn from the National Academy of Sciences issued a report: DNA Technology in Forensic Science, supported with joint funding from the National Institute of Justice, the Federal Bu-

reau of Investigation, and the State Justice Institute, under award #89-IJ-CX-0055 from the National Institute of Justice, Office of Justice Programs, US Department of Justice. See Disclaimer 2vi. "Points of view in this document are those of the authors and do not necessarily represent the official position of the US Department of Justice."

7. The above report (NRC-1 report) at page 70 acknowledges:

"The theory of PCR analysis, 'even though it is the analysis of synthetic DNA, as opposed to the natural sample,' is scientifically accepted and has been accepted by a number of courts." (EX-1) See also EX-1-A and 1-B regarding confidentiality.

See also NRC member Dr. Kazazians false testimony in Gentry EX 1, 1-A, 1-B.

8. In 1993 in State v. Lyons, 863 P2d 1303 at 1309. Footnote 12, the high court omits the portion from the NRC-1 report at page 70. "Even though it is the analysis of synthetic DNA as opposed to the natural sample," with an ellipsis! "This was the first act of withholding material fact that forensic PCR product is in fact not DNA." (EX-2)

9. In 1994 in State v. Russell 882 P2d 747 (WASH 1994), in this case the elephant in the room that was avoided about the general scientific acceptance of PCR testing, that was not distinguished at 793, was that, "PCR's product is 100% extrinsic, synthetic," non-DNA, and that FACT was never addressed beyond: (125 Wn. 2d 101) The quote, the experts and the opinions cited to by the majority all refer to the RFLP technique of DNA identification and not to PCR amplification analysis. The majority states, "The report acknowledges the admissibility of DNA evidence, without distinguishing between the PCR and RFLP methodology," (italics mine), majority, at 46, and then quotes to a section of the report that in fact appears to me to be discussing RFLP and not PCR when it states it is unnecessary to hold admissibility hearings on the scientific techniques. In fact, the missing middle section of the majority's quote, majority, at 46, from pages 145-46 of the report clearly discusses RFLP analysis. Additionally, on the previous page of the report the NRC states that, "…the use of PCR amplification for sample preparation might require a pretrial hearing on the properties of the technique because it introduces a novel issue considered by only a few courts thus far—the synthesis of evidence by amplification." (EX-3)

10. October 11, 1996 in State v. Lyons 924 P.2d 802 (Or Sup Ct). On review from the Court of Appeals (En Banc) concluded that the PCR method generally is accepted as being scientifically valid by the scientific community, including the forensic field. (Noting fn 22) whereat fn 22.

"In 1992, the National Research Counsel noted that 'the theory' of the PCR analysis *** is scientifically accepted and has been accepted by a number of courts."

Fact: The Supreme Court of Oregon intentionally withheld the material fact [that] "even though it is the analysis of 'synthetic DNA' as opposed to the natural sample." From Mr. Robert Wallace Lyons, "Committing extrinsic fraud and concealing intrinsic fraud." EX-4

11. December 18, 1996 in United States v. Reginald Pierce Beasley 102 F3d 1440 (8th Cir 1996), first Federal Circuit Court of Appeals to rule on the admissibility of the PCR method providing "judicial notice." This case makes no reference to the NRC-1 report, nor is J. Gerdes' name mentioned. A Daubert hearing was held in the lower court before the Honorable David S. Doty District Judge. Quoted in full, omitting only the District Court's footnotes, in relevant part here at 1445. It is incorrectly stated that:

"By utilizing the PCR method, one can produce a substantial number of specific segments of human DNA which can then be typed." (EX-5) compare TRALA at 13 infra

"[This] was not an accident or a misspoken word."

12. October 3, 1997 in United States v. Gaines 979 F.Supp 1429 (USDC SD FLA), at 1432 is the only case to cite Beasley at 1445 referring to DNA as "human DNA." Every case since Gaines supra refers to DNA as DNA with no other references to being "human DNA." Further, in Gaines at 1436 DNA Technology in Forensic Science at 5-6 and (NRC-2 1996) Evaluation of Forensic DNA 1996 at 70. "Page numbers are 'transposed' to misdirect readers away from NRC-1 1992 pg 70." (EX-6)

13. September 17, 2001 in United States v. Trala 162 F.Supp.2d 336 (USDC DD) at 341. District Court Judge Gregory M. Sleet cites the QUOTE from Beasley cited in Gaines, but misdirects the reader from Gaines at 1432 to Gaines at 1435 and then, sua sponte, misquotes Beasley at 1445 and Gaines at 1432 with his own rendition at Trala (162 F.Supp.2d 341) quote:

"By using this process, a lab can produce a substantial number of specific, targeted segments of DNA which can then be typed." Compair, Beasley at 11 supra.

"Judge Sleet sua sponte removed the word human from Gaines citing Beasley and misdirected the reader away from the actual quote in Gaines from page 1432 to page 1435." (EX-7)

14. March 21, 2003 in United States v. Ewell 252 F.Supp.2d 104 (USDC Dist NJ) at 115. "The government falsely claims that PCR-STR is 'materially similar' to other forms of DNA typing methods," such as RFLP/VNTR, DQ-Alpha and Polymarker. "PCR 'replicates' testable material from scratch made entirely from the materials supplied in the kits, Profiler Plus and Cofiler or Identifier kits," that include a disclaimer which provides "For research purposes only," and "Not for use in diagnostic systems." PCR-STR and "all other methods that do not employ PCR are distinctly different;" as "PCR 'produces' an inorganic, synthetic, extrinsic, virtual sample that

is 'structurally incomplete'" and factually not "DNA," and is made from "patented proprietary materials" from a "patented materials kit" and ultimately patent eligible as a synthetic creation not normally present in nature. (EX-8) (EX-12)

15. March 16, 2009 in United States v. Davis 602 F.Supp.2nd 658 (2009) Davis cites Gaines but, "uses the 'rendition of Judge Gregory M. Sleet from Trala supra' omitting the word human before the acronym 'DNA'." This case acknowledges co-incidental matches between profiles of "unrelated individuals" found within the Arizona state and Prince George's County, Maryland databases "despite astronomical random match probability calculations." In the prior proceedings in this case, a state court judge ordered the Maryland State Police CODIS Director to search the Maryland DNA database against itself and determine the number of pairs of profiles that matched at nine to 13 Loci. (EX-9)

On January 31, 2007, Maryland CODIS Administrator Michelle Graves produced a declaration indicating that the search indicated 21 matches at nine loci; three matches at 10 loci; one match at 11 loci; four matches at 12 loci; and three matches at 13 loci. A number of these matches were explained by the presence of identical twins or close relatives in the database, but several were between completely unrelated individuals. One individual in the Prince George's County database matched two other unrelated individuals at seven loci, an event that, according to the product rule, produced a RMP of one in one trillion. "Dr. Mueller, upon reviewing this data, opined that the fact that coincidental matches were found in the Prince George's County database of 'less than ten thousand profiles,' shows that statements or inferences of uniqueness can be fundamentally incorrect."

16. In response to the above "coincidental matches" at the Arizona Department of Public Safety Northern Regional Crime Laboratory Flagstaff, Arizona, the Officer of the Inspector General US Department of Justice Audit Division, conducted an audit in February 2015; and after finding (5) of the profiles of the 100 sampled did not meet NDIS requirements. The FBI's NDIS Operational Procedures Manual establishes the DNA data acceptance standards by which laboratories must abide. "Laboratories are prohibited from uploading forensic profiles to NDIS that clearly match the DNA profile of the victim or another known person that is not a suspect." "Such prevalence of coincidental matches is evident of STR invalidity."

17. People v. Pizarro 216 Cal. App. 4th 658; 158 Cal Rptr. 3d55; (2013), Cal. App. LEXIS 402 F057722 May 12, 2013, opinion filed. At 705 Allelic dropout, "As use of various STR kits has become more prevalent." See: Allelic dropout at 703 e.; b. and d. were "depublished" by the Attorney General of the State of California!

Once different manufacturers overcame the monopoly on the industry by the FBI. Kits made by different manufacturers and containing different (proprietary) primer sets, "led to the discovery of null alleles." Fn.49. (EX-10)

18. Now, concordance studies are conducted with different kits to discover more null alleles. If two kits containing different primers produce different (discordant) results from the same person's DNA (one kit producing a heterozygous genotype and the other producing a homozygous genotype), allelic dropout is suspected as the cause of the homozygous genotype.

19. As of May 21, 2013, STR Base lists, for example, eight null allele incidents discovered at the VWA locus alone, four of which occurred using Profiler Plus Kit but not with another kit; loss of allele 19; loss of alleles 15 and 17; loss of allele 16; and loss of alleles 17, 18 and 19. How many were undiscovered?

"It appears courts are uninterested in convictions based on null alleles or false homozygous (discordant) results that [ARE] EXCULPATORY!" (i.e. wrongful convictions).

Fact:

"The STR method can only measure length, not sequence."

The California Appeals Court at 723 exclaims, "If the ultimate test of identity between two DNA samples is the identity of their sequences, then methods that suppress or mask sequence differences may not be appropriate in the criminal context."

The court went on to recommend that the scientific community reexamine the possible effects and management of allelic dropout in criminal cases, but stopped short of ordering any reexamination of any cases.

Pizarro was reversed (216 Cal. App. 4th 724).

Bottom line is, "allelic recovery" in the "criminal context" is, unquestionably, "the manipulation of the evidence."

20. Low Copy Number (LCN)

LCN testing refers to DNA tests done on amounts of DNA that are at or below the "stochastic threshold."

Four problematic effects (stochastic effects) are often seen with testing performed below the stochastic threshold: (1) exaggerated stutter, (2) peak height imbalance, (3) allelic drop-in, and (4) allelic drop-out.

Different laboratories have different stochastic thresholds. Manufacturers of the "evidence kits" recommend 1.0 nanograms for reliable results. There are 1000 picograms in one nanogram.

It is unlikely that any "DNA expert" would know the significance or relevance of LCN to admissibility of the evidence. "The expert attempts to obtain results," he is not concerned that his methods may constitute a legal manipulation or outright fabrication of evidence.

DNA technology in forensic science must be at the highest quality. Instead, it is at the absolutely lowest quality when performed not only below manufacturers' recommended amount, but in many cases below the stochastic threshold set by labs.

21. In an attempt to rescue the STR method after the discovery of null alleles, the "Identifiler Kit" was introduced with "NEW degenerate primers, to eliminate mismatch at primer binding sites." These primers further mask sequence variations at these sites "that can be of exculpatory value."

22. "Labs are using methods to convict, that in turn cannot be used to exonerate," in violation of the Innocence Protection Act 18 USC § 3600a(5). (IPA-2004.)

23. In short, the bottom line is DNA's admissibility lies on an inaccurate factual foundation. Admissibility was initially based on RFLP that PRODUCED HUMAN DNA by digestion with a single restriction enzyme detected/tagged with radioactive phosphorus and nonspecific probe is washed away. The actual fragments are subjected to electrophoresis, transferred to a nylon membrane, placed on an x-ray film and radioactive emissions expose the film, called an autoradiograph or autorad. If two bands were visible on an autorad, the person is heterozygous. But if the bands occur in indistinguishable positions, so that only one is visible, the person is resumed to be homozygous.

24. The distinction between RFLP and PCR is the RFLP analysis required about 50 nanograms of relatively nondegraded DNA. The PCR method is fully manipulable through allelec dropout or drop-in and is a synthetic recreation made entirely from the contents of the "patented proprietary evidence kit," complete with disclaimer! "PCR Product is extrinsic, synthetic, acyclonucleotide product and is structurally different, by adding a label and breaking apart naturally occurring pentose sugar by removing two carbon atoms and their associated oxygen and hydrogen atoms and replacing with non-nucleotide, extrinsic, synthetic patented materials." See: Enzo Biochem, 902 F.Supp.2d 308 (USDC SDNY 2012).

Fact: PCR produces ARTIFICIAL SIMIULATED EVIDENCE. (EX-11)

25. Forensic kits used worldwide, see: Promega @ Lexis, pg 41. "Do not perform an analysis for the identification of individuals." Promega @ Lexis, pg 34, Promega has an exclusive, worldwide license…EXCEPT FOR, "Human linkage analysis in the research genetics field of use." See Promega @ Lexis, pg 31 Promega Corp v. Life Tech, 10-CU-281-bbc (11/29/11) EX-12.

26. Therefore, by legal definition, no "DNA analysis" as defined by 42 USC § 40702(c)(1)(2), NRS 176.09118 of any "DNA sample" as defined by 42 USS § 40702(c)(1), NRS 176.09112 of any DNA "deoxyribonucleic acid" has been, nor ever will be, analyzed via the PCR method in the criminal context.

27. PCR-STR method is unreliable and irrelevant, fake, remanufactured, synthetic, resulting in coincidental matches (at 15) breaking any chain of custody and any alleged probable cause therefrom.

# How the Courts use Fake "DNA" as Evidence When It's Inadmissible

"DNA evidence" used in the courtroom is, 1) not "DNA" and 2) not "direct evidence." It is synthetic biology, not to be confused with organic cloning.

The Polymerase Chain Reaction (PCR) method is a method used to "remanufacture DNA evidence," an enzymatic synthesis made entirely from extrinsic, synthetic materials from a patented materials kit, proprietary in nature.

Material Facts

1. PCR analysis is analysis of synthetic DNA as opposed to the natural sample. See: 1992 NRC-1 Report page 70, DNA Technology in Forensic Science. This report was confidential as of January 6, 1995. Authored by the National Academy of Sciences.

2. The synthetic nature of the PCR method (material fact) was omitted from case law with an ellipsis while referring to the NRC-1 1992 Confidential Report. See: State V. Lyons 924 P.2d 802 at 811-12 and fn 22 (Ore 1996).

3. Fraud was committed in U.S. V. Beasley, 102 F.3d 1440 at 1445 (8th Cir 1996) (First Circuit Court to rule on the admissibility of PCR DNA) USDC Judge David S. Doty, "By utilizing the PCR method one can produce a substantial number of specific segments of human DNA." Providing "judicial notice" for the PCR method.

4. Only two cases in history refer to "human DNA" in regard to the PCR method, Beasley Supra and U.S. V. Gaines, 979 F.Supp 1429 at 1432 citing Beasley (USDC SO FL 1997).

5. United States District Court Judge Gregory m. Sleet in U.S. V. Trala, 162 F.Supp 2d 336 at 341 (D Del 2001) ((changed quoted caselaw with his own words)) omitting

the word HUMAN when quoting Gaines at 1435 instead of Gaines at 1432. Clearly to cover up the fraud in Beasley at 1445.

6. Therefore, by definition and synthetics not being contemplated by State nor Federal statutes: No "DNA analysis" as defined by 42 USC § 14135 a(c)(2), NRS 176.09118 of any "DNA sample" as defined by 42 USC § 14135 a(c)(1), NRS 176.09112 of any "DNA," as defined by NRS 176.09114 "Deoxyribonucleic Acid" has not been, nor ever will be, analyzed by the PCR method in the criminal context.

Re-manufactured, counterfeited, fake evidence is NOT EVIDENCE any more than counterfeit currency is money! Re-manufacturing evidence breaks the chain of custody and may be fruit of the poisonous tree stemming from Beasley Supra.

Short Tandem Repeats (STR) method of DNA detection, commonly referred to as Junk DNA. STRs are not genes, nor do they code for a protein. They are also responsible for what the FBI says are "coincidental matches" in the Arizona and Delaware databases. In fact, the STR method only measures lengths and therefore masks any exculpatory sequence variants and is inappropriate in the criminal context. See: People V. Pizarro, 216 Cal App 4th 658 May 21, 2013.

In fact, new inventions of Genetic Technologies Ltd, assignee of U.S. Patent No. 5,621,179 (179 Patent) and No. 5,851,762 (762 Patent) both cover methods of analyzing noncoding portions of DNA that correlates with certain genetic traits implicating privacy interests and illegal search issues.

The admissibility of DNA technology in forensic science is based on inadequate and inaccurate factual foundation and cannot be reliable opinion, no matter how valid principles and methods applied or how well-qualified expert: Fernandez V. SparTek Indus., 76 Fed R Evid Serv (CBC) 784, 2008 U.S. Dist Lexis 41520 (DSC May 23, 2008); Federal Rules of Evidence 702 and 703. Inadequate and inaccurate factual foundation stems from United States V. (Oliver) Beasley 102 F.3d 1440 at 1445 8th Cir 1996) wherein, providing judicial notice for the (PCR) Polymerase Chain Reaction/DNA Amplification method, falsely states: "By utilizing the PCR method, one can 'produce' a substantial number of specific segments of 'human DNA' which can then be typed." Factually, PCR analysis is the analysis of synthetic DNA as opposed to the natural sample. See: National Research Counsel 1992 Report (NRC-1 Report) DNA Technology in Forensic Science pg 70. THIS WAS NO MISTAKE! After a review of the admissibility, history, caselaw of the PCR method, a clear intent to deceive is revealed. Firstly, within the case law, the word amplify and all variations thereof, are used as a "weasel word" to conceal "synthetic replication." Amplify and replicate are not analogous and have separate meanings. The early methods of DNA analysis such as Restriction Fragment Length Polymorphism (RFLP) was not a physical re-manufacture of evidence like the PCR method. These two methods were never distinguished.

In 1994 in State V. Russell, 125 Wn.2d; 882 P.2d747; 1994 Wash. Lexis 635; 63 U.S.L.W. 2291 No. 60673-1 reveals at 792 "The theory of PCR analysis, even though it is the analysis of synthetic DNA, as opposed to the natural sample, is scientifically accepted and has been accepted by a number of courts." Then, at 793 goes on to state, "Majority," at 45-46 (quoting DNA technology at 70). However, the majority then dismisses this crucial and, I believe, determinative statement of scientific opinion by quoting a section from a later chapter of the report and by concluding that "experts" and a "number of court decisions" refute the challenge to the admissibility of PCR. Majority, at 46-48; See: 125 Wn.2d at 101; the quote, the experts and the court opinions cited to by the majority all refer to the RFLP technique of DNA identification and not to PCR amplification analysis. The majority states, "The report acknowledges the admissibility of DNA evidence, without distinguishing between the PCR and RFLP methodology," majority, at 46, and then quotes to a section of the report that in fact appears to me to be discussing RFLP and not PCR when it states it is unnecessary to hold admissibility hearings on the scientific techniques. In fact, the missing middle section of the majority's quote, majority, at 46, from pages 145-46 of the report clearly discusses RFLP analysis. Additionally, on the previous page of the report, the NRC states that, "The use of PCR amplification for sample preparation might require a pretrial hearing on the properties of the technique, because it introduces a novel issue considered by only a few courts thus far—the 'synthesis of evidence by amplification'." DNA technology, at 144, if page 145 of the report is referring to PCR evidence when it says no hearing is necessary, then it conflicts with the statement about PCR on the prior page. My interpretation is congruent with the report's conclusion that "[t]he current laboratory procedure for detecting DNA variation (specifically, single-locus probes analyzed on southern blots without evidence of band shifting) is fundamentally sound. DNA technology at 149. The parenthetical material describes the RFLP technique of DNA analysis, not PCR analysis. In 1995 in State V. Gentry, 125 Wn.2d 570; 888 P.2d 1105; 1995 Wash. Lexis 2 No. 58415-0 (at 888 P.2d at 1157). The error of concluding PCR has achieved general acceptance in the scientific community for testing on forensic samples was comprehensively set forth in the dissent in State V. Russell, 125 Wn.2d 24, 882 P.2d 747 (1994). The dissent's reasoning in Russell, in which I fully concurred, applies with equal force here. See: 888 P.2d at 1158. See also: 125 Wn.2d at 662 (NRC-1), "1992 report was confidential as of Jan. 6, 1995."

In 1996 in State V. Lyons, 324 Ore 256; 924 P.2d 802; 1996 Ore Lexis 102 SC 541261. Lyons, 924 P.2d at 811-12 and footnote 22, uses an ellipsis omitting material fact/synthetic nature from 1992 NRC-1 report (even though it is the analysis of synthetic DNA, as opposed to the natural sample).

In 1996, United States V. Beasley, 102 F.3d 1440 at 1445 (8th Cir 1996) falsely portrays the PCR method as "producing human DNA" and providing judicial notice for admissibility of the PCR method. FRAUD.

In 1997, United States V. Gaines, 979 F.Supp 1429; 1997 U.S. Dist. Lexis 19445; 48 Fed. R. Evid. Serv. (Callaghan) 419 Case No. 96-6159-CR-GOLD (Oct. 3, 1997) Gaines at 1432 B. Citing Beasley, Supra, is the only other case in history to cite to Beasley at 1445, quoting the quote from Beasley using the word HUMAN when referring to DNA. The word HUMAN is no longer present in case law after Gaines.

In 2001, United States V. Trala, 162 F.Supp.2d.336; 2001 U.S. Dist. Lexis 14572; 57 Fed. R. Evid. Serv. (Callaghan) 1266 Criminal Action No. 00-23-GMS (Sept. 27, 2001) United States District Court Judge Gregory M. Sleet at 341 misquotes and misdirects readers by citing Gaines at 1435, in place of Gaines at 1432, and misquoting the quote in Beasley cited in Gaines with his own quote! "BY USING THIS PROCESS, A LAB CAN PRODUCE A SUBSTANTIAL NUMBER OF SPECIFIC, TARGETED SEGMENTS OF DNA WHICH CAN THEN BE TYPED." Unprecedented!

No federal or state statute defines "DNA" as extrinsic, synthetic, re-manufactured materials, fabricated from a patented materials kit. Science is definitive and in quotations.

No "DNA analysis" as defined by Federal Statute 42 USC § 14135 a(c)(2), state statute NRS.176.09118 of any "DNA sample" as defined by Federal Statute 42 USC § 14135 a(c)(1), state statute NRS.176.09112 of any "DNA" as defined by NRS.176.09114 "deoxyribonucleic acid" is, has, nor ever will be analyzed by the PCR method of synthetic, extrinsic, re-manufactured materials, fabricated from a patented materials kit in the criminal context.

The government knew PCR analysis was the analysis of synthetic DNA as opposed to the natural sample in 1992. The government omitted material fact (D). The government misrepresented (E) and the government covered up at (F). "CLEAR INTENT."

Clearly, the PCR methodology is NOT what it was purported to be, its admissibility is based on inadequate and an inaccurate factual foundation and due to its synthetic, extrinsic nature as re-manufactured, breaks any chain of and/or and finding of probable cause, and represents "fruit of the poisonous tree," and is inadmissible. Federal Rules of Evidence 702 and 703; Fernandez V. SparTek Indus., 76 Fed. R. Evid. Serv. (CBC 784, 2008 U.S. Dist Lexis 41520 (DSC May 23, 2008).

The Biggest Lie by the FBI—Fake DNA

The following facts will prove that everyone has been deceived into believing that "DNA testing" in the criminal context is "DNA," when in reality, "It is as FAKE as a counterfeit dollar bill!"

The Polymerase Chain Reaction (PCR) method is the method used to re-manufacture DNA; a "synthetic FAKE"; made entirely of extrinsic materials from a patented materials kit. The inventor, Dr. Kary B. Mullis and Dr. Richards won the Nobel prize in science for their invention, however, Dr. Mullis has testified that it should not be used in forensics.

It must also be noted that the Short Tandem Repeat (STR) method of detection only measures length(s) and actually masks EXCULPATORY SEQUENCE VARIANTS! (that) can demonstrate exclusion. People V. Pizarro, DE-PUBLISHED by the Attorney General of California "chain of custody and/or finding of probable cause." (cite omitted)

In the early years of DNA technology in forensic science, but for the D1S80 Test; PCR was not used.

When the technology changed to PCR, a re-manufacture of the evidence, by synthetic means, it was called the "synthesis of evidence by amplification." "Amplify" is a "weasel word" for "replicate." See State V. Russell, State V. Gentry. PCR was never distinguished from Restriction Fragment Length Polymorphism (RFLP).

The quote that revealed the "synthetic nature" of the PCR method from the 1992 National Research Counsel Report (NRC-1 1992) (DNA technology in forensic science was largely omitted from case law; see example in State V. Lyons 924 P.2d 802 at 811-12 & (Ore 1996) (Ellipsis omits, "Even though it is the analysis of synthetic DNA, as opposed to the natural sample.") The NRC-1 Report of 1992 was CONFIDENTIAL as of January 6, 1995.

In many of the early admissibility cases, the "defendants did not have experts," and the evidence went unchallenged. Even the first three appellate decisions in this nation, the defendants had no experts. See: Andrew, Coby and Spencer, infra.

The PCR method finally made its way to the Circuit Court in United States V. Beasley, (Oliver) 102 F.3d 1440 at 1445 (8th Cir 1996); "The First Federal Circuit Court to analyze the PCR method" and provides JUDICIAL NOTICE for the method, falsely repeats the lower court's opinion of USDC Judge David S. Doty that at 1445, "By utilizing the PCR method one can produce a substantial number of specific segments of human DNA which can then be typed." That statement is patently false; See: (1992 NRC-1 Report pg. 70) (PCR is analysis of synthetic DNA).

Please note that only two cases in U.S. history (to my knowledge) refer to DNA as "human DNA," Beasley and Gaines that cites Beasley.

United States District Court Judge Gregory M. Sleet, in United States V. Trala, 162 F.Supp 2nd 336 (D. De.2001) at 341, misquoted and misdirected readers when he cited Gaines at 1435 instead of Gaines at 1432 and replaced the quote from Gaines at 1432, citing Beasley with his own quote:

Trala at 341:

"By using this process, a lab can produce a substantial number of specific, targeted segments of DNA which can then be typed."

Judge Sleet sua sponte removed the word "human" that appears in Beasley at 1445 and Gaines at 1432 citing Beasley!

Beasley at 1445:

"By utilizing the PCR method one can 'produce' a substantial number of specific segments of 'human DNA' which can then be typed."

The admissibility of "DNA" in the criminal context is based upon FALSE, INACCURATE, INADEQUATE factual foundation, FRE Rule 702 and 703 follow that an opinion based on "inadequate, inaccurate factual foundation" cannot be reliable opinion, no matter how valid principles and methods applied or how well-qualified the expert. Fernandez V. SparTek Indus, 76 Fed Rules Evid Serv (CBC) 784 2008 U.S. Dist Lexis 41520 DSC May 23, 2008.

The above facts establish beyond any doubt that by definition:

No "DNA analysis" as defined by 42 USC § 14135 a(c)(2), NRS 176.09118 of any "DNA sample" as defined by 42 USC § a(c)(1), NRS 176.09112 of any "DNA", "deoxyribonucleic acid" as defined by NRS 176.09114 is, has, or ever will be analyzed by the PCR method in the criminal context.

The story of deception by the FBI goes to many other issues such as the null alleles database and surely hidden in the FBI's CODIS database along with "proprietary secrets" held in the patent context, exculpatory evidence held secretly by law enforcement, FBI.

This story goes on and on, but I will end here with a final thought. Upon the very first cycle of the thermal cycler/oven, the actual "DNA" is OBLITERATED by heat, then remanufactured with synthetics. This in turn factually breaks the chain of custody and negates any probable cause therefrom. Further, the illegality of Beasley, falsely claiming PCR produces HUMAN DNA, could be seen as FRUIT OF THE POISONOUS TREE; violating due process under the Fourteenth Amendment to the U.S. Constitution.

Counterfeiting is a federal crime, be it currency or EVIDENCE!

December 8, 2019

## TABLE OF AUTHORITIES

1. Andrews V. State, 533 So.2d 841 (Fla. App 1988)
2. Cobey V. State, 80 Md. Appl. 31, 559 A. 2d 391 (1989)
3. Fernandez V. SparTek Indus, U.S. Dist Lexis 41520 (DSC 2008)
4. State V. Gentry, 888 P.2d 1105 (Wash 1995)
5. State V. Lyons, 924 P.2d 802 (Ore Sup Ct 1996)
6. State V. Russell, 882 P.2d 747 (Wash Sup Ct 1994)
7. People V. Pizzaro, 211 Cal. App. 4th 658 May 21, 2013
8. U.S. V. Beasley, 102 F.3d 1440 at 1445 (8th Cir 1996)
9. U.S. V. Trala, 162 F. Supp 2d 336 (D Del 2001)
10. U.S. V. Gaines, 979 F.Supp 1429 (SO FL Oct 3, 1997)
11. 1992 NRC-1 Report
12. Federal Statute 42 USC § 14135 a et seq. CODIS
13. Nevada Revised Statute NRS 176.09112, 09114, 09118
14. Spencer V. Commonwealth, 238 Va. 275, 384 S.E.2d 775 (1989)
15. United States v. Ewell 252 F.Supp.2d 104 (USDC Dist NJ) at 115
16. United States v. Davis 602 F.Supp.2nd 658 (2009)

In 1992, the National Academy of Sciences, Committee on DNA Technology in Forensic Science, including Dr. Haig H. Kazazian, published "DNA Technology in Forensic Science." (1992 NRC Report) at page 70, quote: "The theory of PCR analysis, even though it is the analysis of synthetic DNA, as opposed to the natural sample, is scientifically accepted and has been accepted by a number of courts." (Exhibit-1)

In The State of Washington V. Johnathan Lee Gentry, 125 Wn. 2d 570; 888 P.2d 1105; 1995 WASH LEXIS 2 at 662, in relevant part here. Dr. Haig H. Kazazian "at the time of his testimony he was a member of the National Research Committee of the National Academy of Sciences, which had not released its report on DNA. Because it was confidential, Dr. Kazazian testified he could not reveal its contents." (Exhibit-2). See also; The National Academies Press letter dated September 9, 2020, stating "This report was never classified as confidential." When "DNA Technology in Forensic Science" was released in 1992 it was immediately made available for purchase through our website (Exhibit-3).

It is clear that the synthetic nature of the PCR method was never distinguished from the RFLP method. See Wash V. Russell, 125 Wn 2d at 100-101 (Wash 1994) (Exhibit-4).

The quote from the National Academy of Sciences "DNA Technology in Forensic Science" at page 70 ("Even though it is the analysis of synthetic DNA, as opposed to the natural sample.") was OMITTED with an ellipsis in State of Oregon V. Robert Wallace Lyons, 924 P.2d 802 at 811-812 and fn. 22, (Ore. 1996) (Exhibit-5).

United States District Court Judge David S. Doty in United States District Court District of Minnesota Fourth Division Criminal No. 4-94-127 (1)(2) United States of America, Plaintiff V. Reginald P. Beasley and Oliver Beasley, 102 F.3d 1440 at 1445 (8th Cir. 1996) ("By utilizing the PCR method, one can produce a substantial number of specific segments of human DNA which can then be typed.") Judge David S. Doty has a background in biology and knew that the PCR method DOES NOT PRODUCE HUMAN DNA (Exhibit-6)!

The FRAUD committed in Beasley, supra was furthered by Gregory M. Sleet, United States District Court Judge, District of Delaware, in United States of America, Plaintiff V. John Walter Trala and Melissa Bailey, 162 F.Supp. 2d 336; 2001 US Dist. Lexis 14572; 57 Fed R. Evid. Serv (3d Cir. Del. 2004). Misdirected and misquoted at 341—Gaines at 1435 in place of Gaines at 1432 and changing the quote from Beasley with his own words in place of Beasley at 1445, compare Trala at 341 (Exhibit-7). See also, Gaines (Exhibit-8).

Beasley at 1445

"By utilizing the PCR method one can produce a substantial number of specific segments of HUMAN DNA which can then be typed."

Trala at 341

"By using this process, a lab can produce a substantial number of specific, targeted segments of DNA which can then be typed."

F. FINCH

# INDEX OF EXHIBITS

# Exhibit 1

Description: "DNA Technology in Forensic Science" (1992 NRC-1 Report) National Research Council pg. 70.

# DNA Technology in Forensic Science

Committee on DNA Technology in Forensic Science
Board on Biology
Commission on Life Sciences
National Research Council

NATIONAL ACADEMY PRESS
Washington, D.C. 1992

loci. It generates a large quantity of relatively pure product that can be analyzed with much greater precision than Southern blots, even down to the nucleotide level. At the same time, it poses even more serious issues of proficiency, control, and technology transfer than RFLP typing.

In summary, it is well established that one can greatly amplify a locus with authenticity and that one can reliably detect alleles or sequence variation at the amplified locus with any of a number of techniques. PCR analysis is extremely powerful in medical technology, but it has not yet achieved full acceptance in the forensic setting. The theory of PCR analysis, even though it is the analysis of synthetic DNA, as opposed to the natural sample, is scientifically accepted and has been accepted by a number of courts. However, most forensic laboratories have invested their energy in development of RFLP technology and have left the development of forensic PCR technology to a few other laboratories. Thus, there is no broad base of experience in the use of the technique in identity testing.

Forensic PCR-based testing is now limited for the most part to analysis of genetic variation at the DQ locus in the HLA complex. Potential ambiguities in typing results cannot yet be checked by studying a number of other loci in the same DNA sample. That shortcoming will be rectified with the addition of new PCR markers for forensic analysis. However, it is clear that analysis of the DQ locus with PCR can often provide useful information during the investigative phase in the forensic setting.

In general, further experience should be gained with respect to PCR in identity testing. Information on the extent of the contamination problem in PCR analysis and the differential amplification of mixed samples needs to be further developed and published. A great deal of this information can be obtained when a number of polymorphic systems are available for PCR analysis. Ambiguous results obtained with a number of polymorphic markers will signal contamination or mixtures of DNA in a sample.

Quantification of PCR results needs to be explored, to make the results more reliable. Laboratories that gain experience with PCR should determine the relationship between cycle number and percentage of contaminating DNA easily detected for each system used. Control primers that amplify small amounts of DNA reliably and robustly need to be added to test amplifications. In general, information derived from new polymorphic loci under standardized conditions with easily quantifiable results or end points is needed. Considerable advances in the use of PCR in forensic analysis can be expected soon; the method has enormous promise.

## NATIONAL COMMITTEE ON FORENSIC DNA TYPING

Forensic DNA typing is advancing rapidly. RFLP-based typing methods continue to be refined and improved, PCR typing methods are being

## Exhibit 2

Description: State v. Gentry, 125 Wn. 2d 570 at 662 (1995 Wash) Dr. Haig Kazazian testified the 1992 NRC-1 Report was confidential.

THE STATE OF WASHINGTON, Respondent, v. JONATHAN LEE GENTRY, Appellant.
SUPREME COURT OF WASHINGTON
125 Wn.2d 570; 888 P.2d 1105; 1995 Wash. LEXIS 2
No. 58415-0
January 6, 1995, Filed

Editorial Information: Subsequent History

As Corrected January 25, 1995. Writ of certiorari denied Gentry v. Washington, 516 U.S. 843, 116 S. Ct. 131, 133 L. Ed. 2d 79, 1995 U.S. LEXIS 5810 (1995)Post-conviction relief denied at In re Personal Restraint of Gentry, 137 Wn.2d 378, 972 P.2d 1250, 1999 Wash. LEXIS 126 (1999)Writ of habeas corpus denied, Summary judgment denied by Gentry v. Morgan, 2006 U.S. Dist. LEXIS 61069 (W.D. Wash., Aug. 28, 2006)Habeas corpus proceeding at Brown v. Vail, 623 F. Supp. 2d 1241, 2009 U.S. Dist. LEXIS 18741 (W.D. Wash., 2009)Related proceeding at Brown v. Vail, 169 Wn.2d 318, 237 P.3d 263, 2010 Wash. LEXIS 630 (2010)Post-conviction relief denied at In re Pers. Restraint of Gentry, 170 Wn.2d 711, 245 P.3d 766, 2010 Wash. LEXIS 1106 (2010)Post-conviction relief dismissed at In re Pers. Restraint of Gentry, 179 Wn.2d 614, 316 P.3d 1020, 2014 Wash. LEXIS 67 (2014)Related proceeding at State v. Gentry, 2014 Wash. LEXIS 450 (Wash., June 6, 2014)Post-conviction relief denied at State v. Gentry, 2015 Wash. LEXIS 891 (Wash., Aug. 20, 2015)Stay granted by, Post-conviction proceeding at In re Pers. Restraint of Gentry, 2015 Wash. LEXIS 1160 (Wash., Oct. 2, 2015)Summary

Nature of Action: Prosecution for aggravated first degree murder and felony murder.
Superior Court: The Superior Court for Kitsap County, No. 88-1-00395-3, Terence Hanley, J., on July 26, 1991, entered a judgment on a verdict of guilty of both charges and a sentence of death.
Supreme Court: Holding that evidence of various blood tests was properly admitted, that there was sufficient evidence of premeditation and of the aggravating circumstance of concealing identity, that three search warrants were supported by probable cause, that autopsy photographs were properly admitted, that racism did not deny the defendant a fair trial, that the instructions in both the guilt and penalty phases were correct, that the replacement of a juror with an alternate juror did not require reversal, that issues regarding pretrial motions are moot, that testimony of the victim's father and evidence of the defendant's criminal record were properly admitted during the penalty phase, that the trial court's excusal of two prospective jurors was proper, that the prosecutor's arguments did not warrant reversal, and that the death sentence was properly imposed, the court *affirms* the conviction and the death sentence.

CASE SUMMARY

PROCEDURAL POSTURE: The Superior Court for Kitsap County (Washington) convicted defendant of premeditated first-degree murder and felony murder. The trial court sentenced defendant to death, and defendant appealed.DNA and blood test results were admissible in a capital murder case, as they were generally accepted in the scientific community. Victim impact evidence was also admissible under the federal and Washington state constitutions and the state statute.

OVERVIEW: Defendant was convicted of the murder of a 12-year-old girl. The evidence against him

The following scientists testified for the State: Haig H. Kazazian, Jr., M.D., Henry A. Erlich, Ph.D., Stephen P. Daiger, Ph.D., Cecilia Hlavaty von Beroldingen, Ph.D., and Edward T. {125 Wn.2d 662} Blake, Ph.D. For the defense were Aimee Bakken, Ph.D., Ashok Bhagwat, Ph.D., and Mr. David Adler. An affidavit from Dr. Richard Roberts was also admitted.

Dr. Haig Kazazian, Jr., director of the Center for Medical Genetics at Johns Hopkins, had used PCR for medical diagnosis but had never tested crime scene evidence. He testified that PCR can be used on degraded and old samples. He stated he had reviewed the Cetus Corporation's PCR kit, which he had not used, and that the procedures would be generally accepted in the scientific community. 10 Report of Proceedings, at 280; 11 Report of Proceedings, at 444-45.

Dr. Kazazian reviewed Dr. Blake's conclusions and stated the results appeared to be accurate. 10 Report of Proceedings, at 292-93. At the time of his testimony he was a member of the National Research Committee of the National Academy of Sciences, which had not released its report on DNA. Because it was confidential, Dr. Kazazian testified he could not reveal its contents but that to the best of his knowledge there was a consensus of the committee on the use of the Cetus DQ-alpha technology for forensic purposes. 10 Report of Proceedings, at 247, 250.

Dr. Roberts, a molecular biologist, has worked with DNA since 1972 and was the assistant director for research at Cold Spring Harbor in New York. His affidavit concluded that there is not a generally accepted method to assure the PCR amplification is of the product sought to be amplified rather than of a contaminant. He concluded that "at our present state of knowledge, or ignorance, it would be imprudent to rely upon data obtained solely by the PCR method." He also reviewed the PCR testing Dr. Blake performed in this case and concluded he could not agree with Dr. Blake that the shoelace bloodstains unequivocally showed a genotype of 1.2, 3, because there was contamination in the control which showed a 1.1 allele. Ex. 15 (Frye).

Dr. Henry A. Erlich is a geneticist and director of the Human Genetics Department at Cetus Corporation, and has been used as an expert in other criminal trials. 11 Report of Proceedings, at 471, 466; 12 Report of Proceedings, at 496. {125 Wn.2d 663} He testified that PCR is reliable if the person understands the principles of PCR, carries out the reactions carefully and knows how to interpret the data. 12 Report of Proceedings, at 543.

The trial court admitted for cross examination purposes an affidavit written by C. Thomas Casey, M.D., the chairman of the Institute for Molecular Genetics at Baylor College of Medicine and the medical director of a DNA diagnostic laboratory at Baylor. His affidavit was written in October 1989 for use in the *McSherry* case. *People v. McSherry*, 11 Cal. App. 4th 1157, 14 Cal. Rptr. 2d 630 (1992) (ordered withdrawn from publication in official reporter). His affidavit concludes PCR testing is new, not yet validated, and that the testing result excluding the defendant, McSherry, as a source of the DNA was incorrect. Dr. Erlich testified he thought Dr. Casey had changed some of his opinions {888 P.2d 1159} since writing the *McSherry* affidavit. 13 Report of Proceedings, at 711.

An affidavit from Dr. Kenneth K. Kidd, professor of genetics, biology and psychiatry at Yale University School of Medicine, concluded he was unaware of any literature that addresses the problems of PCR evidence in the forensic context.

Dr. Edward T. Blake, a forensic serologist with a doctorate in criminology who has previously testified regarding PCR-DNA evidence, performed the PCR tests in this case. He typed the blood on both of Gentry's shoelaces. In the first testing, conducted July 1989, he was unable to obtain any DNA typing because the material removed from the shoelaces inhibited the amplification reaction, 20 Report of Proceedings, at 1286-88; Ex. 4, at 3 (Frye). However, when he ran PCR tests again in April 1990, he concluded that the genotype on each shoelace was 1.2, 3, consistent with the genotype of the victim. 13 Report of Proceedings, at 853; 20 Report of Proceedings, at 1288, 1221; Ex. 4 (Frye).

# Exhibit 3

Description: The National Academies Press correspondence dated September 9, 2020 confirming the 1992 publication titled "DNA Technology in Forensic Science." This report was never classified as confidential.

# THE NATIONAL ACADEMIES PRESS

Customer Service Department

September 9, 2020

Dear Mr. Frank Peck

First of all I would like to thank you for your interest in our reports. I received your letter regarding our 1992 publication titled "*DNA Technology in Forensic Science*". This report was never classified as confidential. When "*DNA Technology in Forensic Science*" was released in 1992 it was immediately made available for purchase through our website.

The full report is available free at www.nap.edu . The direct link for this report is: (https://www.nap.edu/catalog/1866/dna-technology-in-forensic-science). I am not sure if that is an option within your facility, but perhaps someone on the outside can follow up. While we do not have stock on hand, this report is also available as a reprint through our publication-on-demand program. If you need a copy we can see what options are available.

Should you have any further questions please feel free to contact me at any time. Due to Covid-19 most of us are working from home. We do go into the office about once or twice a month so contact via mail will definitely work for you. At this point we do not expect any changes before the end of the year.

Again, let us know if you have any other questions or concerns.

Kind Regards,

Zina

Zina Jones
National Academies Press
Customer Service Manager
zjones@nas.edu
202-334-3116

*The National Academies of*
SCIENCES · ENGINEERING · MEDICINE

500 Fifth Street, NW, Keck 360, Washington, DC 20001
Phone 202.334.3313  Fax 202.334.2451  E-mail zjones@nas.edu  www.nap.edu

# Exhibit 4

Description: State v. Russell, 125 Wn. 2d 24 at 100-101 (1994 Wash) (PCR method was not distinguished from RFLP method).

> THE STATE OF WASHINGTON, Respondent, v. GEORGE W. RUSSELL, Appellant.
> SUPREME COURT OF WASHINGTON
> 125 Wn.2d 24; 882 P.2d 747; 1994 Wash. LEXIS 635; 63 U.S.L.W. 2291
> No. 60673-1
> October 13, 1994, Filed Summary

Nature of Action: The defendant was charged with murdering three women.
Superior Court: The Superior Court for King County, No. 91-1-00182-7, Patricia H. Aitken, J., on November 27, 1991, entered a judgment on a verdict finding the defendant guilty of two counts of aggravated first degree murder and one count of first degree murder.
Supreme Court: Holding that the polymerase chain reaction (PCR) amplification system for testing DNA at the HLA DQ alpha locus is generally accepted in the relevant scientific community, that evidence derived from a statement made by the defendant before he received *Miranda* warnings was not subject to suppression, that the trial court did not abuse its discretion in refusing to sever the counts, that testimony regarding the rarity of posed murder victims was admissible, that evidence of other suspects and crimes was properly excluded, that certain physical evidence was admissible, that the State's improper cross examination and closing argument did not require a mistrial, and that an accumulation of errors did not deprive the defendant of a fair trial, the court *affirms* the judgment.

CASE SUMMARY

PROCEDURAL POSTURE: Defendant sought review of the order of the Superior Court for King County (Washington), which entered judgment on a verdict finding defendant guilty of two counts of aggravated first-degree murder and one count of first-degree murder. Defendant's murder conviction was upheld because the principles and methodology underlying polymerase chain reaction analysis were found to be generally accepted by the scientific community; thus, the trial court properly admitted DNA test results.

OVERVIEW: Defendant was found guilty of two counts of aggravated first-degree murder and one count of first-degree murder. On appeal, the court affirmed the convictions. The court held that the scientific community generally accepted the principles and methodology underlying the polymerase chain reaction (PCR) amplification system for testing DNA at the DQ alpha locus. Therefore, the court affirmed the admission of the test results, but cautioned that serious flaws in a given test might render PCR evidence unreliable and, thus, inadmissible pursuant to Wash. R. Evid. 702. The court also held that the trial court properly admitted physical evidence derived from an un-Mirandized statement because the statement itself was not coerced. The court identified no abuse of discretion in the trial court's rulings regarding joinder, the admission of evidence on the rarity of posed murder victims, or the exclusion of evidence of other suspects and crimes. The court affirmed the trial court's rulings admitting condoms, a scanner, and a handbook because the trial court evaluated each item's relationship to the issues in the case and fully considered the restrictions of Wash R. Evid. 404, 403, and 404.

OUTCOME: The court affirmed defendant's convictions for murder, holding that the polymerase chain reaction amplification system for testing DNA at the DQ alpha locus was generally accepted in the relevant scientific community and, therefore, the test results could be admitted in court. An un-Mirandized statement by defendant was not coerced and, thus, the evidence derived from said statement was properly admitted.

Prospects of PCR-Based Methods

PCR analysis has a number of desirable features for forensic applications. . . . *At the same time, it poses even more serious issues of proficiency, control, and technology transfer than RFLP typing.*

In summary, it is well established that one can greatly amplify a locus with authenticity and that one can reliably detect alleles or sequence variation at the amplified locus with any of a number of techniques. *PCR analysis is extremely powerful in medical technology, but it has not yet achieved full acceptance in the forensic setting.* The theory of PCR analysis, even though it is the <u>analysis of synthetic DNA, as opposed to the natural sample</u>, is scientifically accepted and has been accepted by a number of courts. *However, most forensic laboratories have invested their energy in development of RFLP technology and have left the development of forensic PCR technology to a few other laboratories. Thus, there is no broad base of experience in the use of the technique in identity testing.*

{125 Wn.2d 100} Forensic PCR-based testing is now limited for the most part to analysis of genetic variation at the DQ [alpha] locus in the HLA complex. *Potential ambiguities in typing results cannot yet be checked by studying a number of other loci in the same DNA sample.* That shortcoming will be rectified with the addition of new PCR markers for forensic analysis. However, it is clear that analysis of the DQ locus with PCR can often provide useful information during the *investigative* phase in the forensic setting.

In general, further experience should be gained with respect to PCR in identity testing. *Information on the extent of the contamination problem in PCR analysis and the differential amplification of mixed samples needs to be further developed and {882 P.2d 793} published.* A great deal of this information can be obtained when a number of polymorphic systems are available for PCR analysis. Ambiguous results obtained with a number of polymorphic markers will signal contamination or mixtures of DNA in a sample.

*Quantification of PCR results needs to be explored, to make the results more reliable.* Laboratories that gain experience with PCR should determine the relationship between cycle number and percentage of contaminating DNA easily detected for each system used. *Control primers that amplify small amounts of DNA reliably and robustly need to be added to test amplifications.* In general, information derived from new polymorphic loci under standardized conditions with easily quantifiable results or end points is needed. *Considerable advances in the use of PCR in forensic analysis can be expected soon; the method has enormous promise.*(Italics mine.) DNA Technology, at 63-70.

The majority recognizes that the NRC report states that the PCR analysis "has not yet achieved full acceptance in the forensic setting", that "there is no broad base of experience in the use of the technique in identity testing", and that "information on the extent of the contamination problem in PCR analysis and the differential amplification of mixed samples needs to be further developed and published." Majority, at 45-46 (quoting *DNA Technology*, at 70). However, the majority then dismisses this crucial and, I believe, determinative statement of scientific opinion by quoting a section from a later chapter of the report and by concluding that "experts" and a "number of court decisions" refute the challenge to the admissibility of PCR. Majority, at 46-48.

{125 Wn.2d 101} The quote, the experts and the court opinions cited to by the majority all refer to the RFLP technique of DNA identification and *not* to PCR amplification analysis.

The majority states "the report acknowledges the admissibility of DNA evidence, *without distinguishing between the PCR and RFLP methodology*" (italics mine), majority, at 46, and then quotes to a section of the report that in fact appears to me to be discussing RFLP and not PCR when it states it is unnecessary to hold admissibility hearings on the scientific techniques. In fact, the missing middle section of the majority's quote, majority, at 46, from pages 145-46 of the report clearly discusses RFLP analysis. Additionally, on the previous page of the report, the NRC states that "[t]he use of PCR amplification for sample preparation might require a pretrial hearing on the properties of the technique, because it introduces a novel issue considered by only a few courts thus far -- the synthesis of evidence by amplification." *DNA Technology*, at 144. If page 145 of the report is referring to PCR evidence when it says no hearing is necessary, then it conflicts with the statement about PCR on the prior page. My interpretation is congruent with the report's conclusion that "[t]he *current laboratory procedure* for detecting DNA variation (specifically, single-locus probes analyzed on Southern blots without evidence of band shifting) is fundamentally sound, . . ." (italics mine.) *DNA Technology*, at 149. The parenthetical material describes the RFLP technique of DNA analysis, not PCR analysis. 29

# Exhibit 5

Description: State v. Lyons, 924 P.2d 802 at 811-12 (1996 Ore) (PCR's synthetic nature omitted with an ellipsis).

> STATE OF OREGON, Respondent on Review, v. ROBERT WALLACE LYONS, Petitioner on Review.
> SUPREME COURT OF OREGON
> 324 Ore. 256; 924 P.2d 802; 1996 Ore. LEXIS 102
> SC S41261
> January 10, 1995, Argued and submitted; July 8, 1996, reassigned
> October 11, 1996, Filed

Editorial Information: Prior History

CC 10-89-08273; CA A68348. On review from the Court of Appeals. *.

Appeal from Lane County Circuit Court, Gregory G. Foote, Judge. 124 Ore. App. 598, 863 P.2d 1303 (1993).

Disposition:
> The decision of the Court of Appeals is affirmed. The judgment of the circuit court is remanded for entry of amended judgment merging murder counts for purposes of conviction and sentence; otherwise affirmed.

CounselSally L. Avera, Public Defender, Salem, argued the cause on behalf of petitioner on review. With her on the petition was David K. Allen, Deputy Public Defender.

Janet A. Klapstein, Assistant Attorney General, Salem, argued the cause on behalf of respondent on review. With her on the brief were Theodore R. Kulongoski, Attorney General, and Virginia L. Linder, Solicitor General.

Judges: Before, Carson, Chief Justice, and Gillette, Van Hoomissen, Fadeley, Graber, and Durham, Justices. **

CASE SUMMARY

PROCEDURAL POSTURE: Petitioner sought review of an order from the Court of Appeals (Oregon), which affirmed the trial court's decision that convicted petitioner for aggravated murder, murder, and burglary in the first degree in violation of Or. Rev. Stat. §§ 163.095, 163.115, and 164.225. The court reviewed the important issue of first impression in the court, the admissibility of polymerase chain reaction (PCR) based DNA evidence. Polymerase chain reaction-based DNA evidence was properly admitted where the trial court satisfied the requisite evaluations of the evidence; defendant failed to seek to test or retest the preserved evidence and the convictions were proper.

OVERVIEW: Petitioner was convicted of aggravated murder, murder, and burglary in the first degree. On appeal, petitioner claimed that the trial court erred in admitting polymerase chain reaction (PCR) based DNA evidence from tests on the hair and saliva samples that were taken from the victim's body and from petitioner. The lower court affirmed and the court addressed the DNA issue as one of first impression. The court evaluated the Oregon Evidence Code and case law from other jurisdictions involving DNA admissibility as well as the analysis of DNA and PCR replication. The court concluded that the PCR method had general acceptance in the forensic field. The court noted that petitioner failed to seek to conduct the independent testing or retesting of the forensic samples after both processed and unprocessed forensic samples were preserved for defense testing and retesting. The court held that the trial court correctly applied the principles laid down in case law and that the trial court did not err in admitting PCR-based DNA evidence. The court declined to address the issue of access to unprivileged material. The court affirmed, but remanded for merger of the murder convictions.

**OUTCOME:** The court affirmed the order of the lower court that affirmed petitioner's convictions for aggravated murder, murder, and burglary in the first degree. The court approved the trial court's admission of the state's polymerase chain reaction (PCR) based DNA evidence. The court remanded for merger of the murder counts for purposes of conviction and sentence.

22

In 1992, the National Research Council noted that "the theory of PCR analysis *** is scientifically accepted and has been accepted by a number of courts." NRC (1992) at 70. In 1996, the National Research Council reported that "the technology for DNA profiling and the methods for estimating frequencies and related statistics have progressed to the point where the reliability and validity of properly collected and analyzed DNA data should not be in doubt." NRC (1996) at ES-1.

# Exhibit 6

Description: United States v. Beasley, 102 F.3d 1440 at 1445 (8th Cir 1996) (by utilizing the PCR method, one can produce a substantial number of specific segments of HUMAN DNA which can then be typed).

   i. Description: Testimony @Beasleys' Daubert Hearing (Pages 3)

   ii. Description: Dr. Richard Roberts' assertion he never (Pages 1) held the position against PCR's application to forensics, dated March 6, 2021, New England Bio Labs.

> United States of America, Appellee, v. Reginald Pierre Beasley, Appellant. United States of America, Appellee, v. Oliver Lawrence Beasley, Appellant.
> UNITED STATES COURT OF APPEALS FOR THE EIGHTH CIRCUIT
> 102 F.3d 1440; 1996 U.S. App. LEXIS 33000
> No. 95-3362, No. 95-3510
> June 12, 1996, Submitted
> December 18, 1996, Filed

Editorial Information: Subsequent History

The Docket Number of this Case has been Corrected by the Court December 27, 1996. Rehearing and Suggestion for Rehearing En Banc Denied January 22, 1997, Reported at: 1997 U.S. App. LEXIS 995. Certiorari Denied May 27, 1997, Reported at: 1997 U.S. LEXIS 3352.

Editorial Information: Prior History

Appeals from the United States District Court for the District of Minnesota. CR 4-94-127, CR 4-94-127-02. Honorable David S. Doty, District Judge.

Disposition:
AFFIRMED.

Counsel           Counsel who presented argument on behalf of appellant Reginald Beasley was Paul Engh of Minneapois, Minnesota. Counsel who presented argument on behalf of appellant Oliver Beasley was L. Marshall Smith of St. Paul, Minnesota.
Counsel who presented argument on behalf of the appellee was Michael W. Ward of Minneapolis, Minnesota. Also appearing on the brief was Mark D. Larsen.

Judges: Before BOWMAN, HEANEY, and BEAM, Circuit Judges.

CASE SUMMARY

PROCEDURAL POSTURE: The United States District Court for the District of Minnesota convicted defendants of conspiring to commit bankruptcy, armed bank robbery, and use of a firearm in a crime of violence. Both defendants appealed their convictions. The court determined that the reliability of the polymerase chain reaction (PCR) method of DNA analysis was sufficiently well established to permit the court to take judicial notice of it.

OVERVIEW: Defendants allegedly committed two bank robberies. One of the defendants argued that the district court erred in admitting DNA evidence of hairs found in a mask, allegedly worn during the commission of the robberies. The court determined that the district court did not abuse its discretion in admitting the evidence. The court also found that the district court properly denied defendant's motion to sever. Both defendants argued that a letter admitted into evidence was hearsay and improperly bolstered a government witness' testimony. The court reasoned that even if the evidence was hearsay, the overwhelming evidence of defendants' guilt rendered the error harmless. Furthermore, the court determined that the evidence was sufficient to support defendants' convictions.

OUTCOME: The court affirmed defendants' convictions.

First, we address the arguments made only by Oliver Beasley.

A.

Oliver Beasley argues that the District Court erred in admitting DNA evidence {102 F.3d 1445} of two hairs found in the "old man" mask worn during the TCF robbery. The mask was left in the getaway car when, following the TCF robbery, the suspects fled the car on foot. Before trial, the District Court conducted an evidentiary hearing concerning the admissibility of DNA evidence using the polymerase chain reaction (PCR) method of DNA typing. At the close of this hearing, the District Court found the evidence admissible. At trial, a government witness, utilizing the PCR technique of DNA analysis, testified that the PCR analysis indicated that the DNA profile of the hair found in the mask matched that of the hair of Oliver Beasley. Beasley contends that PCR testing does not meet the standards of admissibility established by *Daubert v. Merrell Dow Pharmaceuticals, Inc.*, 509 U.S. 579, 125 L. Ed. 2d 469, 113 S. Ct. 2786 (1993), and that even if PCR testing did meet those standards, the protocol and procedures at the Minnesota Bureau of Criminal Apprehension Forensic Science Laboratory (BCA Lab) were not adequate.

The standard of review for a trial court's decisions regarding the admissibility of evidence, including DNA evidence, is abuse of discretion. *See United States v. Johnson*, 56 F.3d 947, 952 (8th Cir. 1995). This Court has already taken judicial notice of the reliability of the general theory and techniques of DNA profiling, and specifically the use of the restriction fragment length polymorphism (RFLP) procedure. *See United States v. Martinez*, 3 F.3d 1191, 1197 (8th Cir. 1993) (citing *United States v. Jakobetz*, 955 F.2d 786, 799-800 (2d Cir.), *cert. denied*, 506 U.S. 834, 121 L. Ed. 2d 63, 113 S. Ct. 104 (1992)), *cert. denied*, 510 U.S. 1062, 114 S. Ct. 734, 126 L. Ed. 2d 697 (1994). 3 The PCR method, however, has not previously been reviewed by this Court. Thus, the District Court appropriately held an evidentiary hearing under standards announced in *Daubert* to determine whether the PCR method is reliable and whether the proffered DNA evidence would be admitted. *See id.*

At the *Daubert* hearing, which consumed more than three days, the District Court heard expert witnesses for both the government and the defense and received numerous exhibits. Based on the evidence adduced at the hearing, the court, having considered defendant's objections to the government's proffered DNA evidence, found the evidence admissible. In its written order, the court carefully set forth its particularized findings regarding the PCR method of DNA typing. These findings provide a concise summary of this method of DNA testing, and we quote them in full, omitting only the District Court's footnotes.

> The PCR method is based upon the natural DNA replication process. By utilizing the PCR method, one can produce a substantial number of specific segments of human DNA which can then be typed. Because 99 percent of the DNA molecule is the same for every individual, the DNA segments amplified for purposes of PCR DNA typing are ones which exhibit genetic variation within the population. These variations provide the basis for DNA typing.

> The PCR method recognizes that the base pairs along the DNA molecule are joined by hydrogen bonds which can be broken by heating. When exposed to heating, the two complementary strands of DNA separate or "denature." Because the bases on a DNA strand are always complementary, a denatured DNA strand forms a template that allows the manufacture of a new strand that is identical to the former complementary strand. This denatured strand is then exposed to two synthetic primers, each complementing a sequence at one end of the target sequence and which bind with their complementary sequences on the separated strands. One of a type of enzymes called polymerase can be used to attach a free nucleotides [sic] to the end of the primer.

D. BING　　　　　　　　　　　DAUB I-183

1　disease assay we didn't, and in the carrier disease diagnostic
2　testing we don't use it either.
3　Q　There have been some, in fact quite a few instances where
4　a forensic lab has been so overcome with PCR contamination
5　that it had to build new laboratories.
6　　　Right?
7　A　If you are referring to my experience, that is right.
8　It wasn't a whole new laboratory. Just a section.
9　Q　Didn't you testify in Leach that there was a laboratory
10　right here in the state of Minnesota, when faced with
11　background PCR contamination which could not be eradicated,
12　changed the gene they were using in their test and they built
13　a whole new building.
14　　　Is that accurate?
15　A　I didn't testify to that. That may be somebody else in
16　the case who testified to that, but I didn't testify to that.
17　I don't know about that.
18　Q　Isn't it true that the NRC has come out and said that PCR
19　testing is not yet fully accepted in the scientific community
20　for forensics and that nothing has changed in the intervening
21　years to change that opinion?
22　　　Isn't that the NRC position?
23　A　They stated that in 1992, that is right.
24　Q　And isn't it true that many prominent scientists have
25　determined that PCR testing is not acceptable for use in

1  forensics?

2  A   That is their opinion. To the best of my knowledge, all
3  the scientists who have said that, have articulated that
4  opinion, are not scientists who run forensic laboratories.

5  Q   Well, isn't it true that two Nobel prize laurettes, Dr.
6  Richard Roberts and Dr. Cary Mullis, who actually invented PCR
7  testing, maintain that position that PCR test testing should
8  not be used in for forensics?

9  A   Yes, they maintain that position, but they don't run
10 forensic laboratories.

11 Q   In other words, they don't make money doing it?

12 A   Oh, that is not true. Dr. Roberts is head of New England
13 Bio Labs, one of the most profitable biotech companies in the
14 United States, and Dr. Roberts makes a lot of money doing
15 molecular biology.

16 Q   Nevertheless, Dr. Roberts, who in fact is a frequent
17 prosecution witness, right?, in DNA RFLP cases and a Noble
18 prize laurette, has said PCR should not be used in the
19 forenisc mode in criminal cases.

20     Correct?

21 A   It is my understanding that he has testified to that, it
22 is my understanding.

23 Q   And again Cary Mullis, who invented PCR testing is also
24 opposed to using PCR DNA testing in forensics?

25 A   Yes, he has testified in California to that.

D. BING  DAUB I-185

1  Q  And I could name probably, what, fifteen or twenty
2  others.
3  Right?
4  A  Well, I could probably name fifteen to twenty others --
5  well I don't know --
6  Q  -- who are opposed to using --
7  A  Well, I don't know about fifteen, but four or five.
8  Q  Okay, who are opposed to using PCR DNA analysis in
9  criminal cases.
10  Right?
11  A  Yes. There is a body of -- there is an opinion in the
12  scientific community that PCR testing should not be used for
13  forensics, that is true.
14  Q  This kit that we talked about was developed by I believe
15  Dr. Blake, Dr. Higuchi, Dr. Sensobau and Dr. Erlich?
16  A  No. The kit was developed by the Cetus Corporation. The
17  people from the Cetus Corporation who were principals in
18  developing the kit were Dr. Higuchi and Dr. Erlich.
19  Dr. Blake has a private laboratory called Forensic
20  Science Associates, and participated in early studies on PCR,
21  was the first laboratory to really use it for forensic
22  analysis.
23  Dr. Sensobau is a professor of criminalistics at
24  University of California in Berkeley, and he participated in
25  the studies as well.

**NEW ENGLAND BioLabs Inc.**

240 County Road  Tel: 978-927-5054  www.neb.com
Ipswich, MA 01938  Fax: 978-921-1350  info@neb.com

R.J. Roberts / Direct line: 978-380-7405 / Fax: 978-338-0660 / email: roberts@neb.com

March 6th, 2021

Frank M. Peck
HDSP Box 650
Indian Springs, NV 89070

Dear Mr. Peck:

I don't know where you came across this statement that Kary Mullis and I maintained that PCR should not be used in forensics, but it is contrary to the position that both Kary (no longer with us) or myself have ever taken.

Speaking for myself, I am both in favor and enthusiastic about using PCR for forensic purposes.

Good luck with your appeal.

Yours sincerely,

Sir Richard Roberts Ph.D., F.R.S.
1993 Nobel Laureate in Physiology or Medicine
Chief Scientific Officer, New England Biolabs
240 County Road Ipswich, MA 01938-2723 USA
Tel: (978) 380-7405 / Fax: (978) 338-0660
Email: roberts@neb.com

# Exhibit 7

Description: United States v. Trala, 162 F.Supp 2d 336 at 341 (U.S. Dist Delaware 2001) Federal District Court Judge Gregory M. Sleet misdirects the reader, citing Gaines, (see: Ex-8) to page 1435 instead of page 1432 and changes the quote from Beasley with his own words, omitting the word HUMAN!

F. FINCH

> UNITED STATES OF AMERICA, Plaintiff, v. JOHN WALTER TRALA, and MELISSA BAILEY, Defendants.
> UNITED STATES DISTRICT COURT FOR THE DISTRICT OF DELAWARE
> 162 F. Supp. 2d 336; 2001 U.S. Dist. LEXIS 14572; 57 Fed. R. Evid. Serv. (Callaghan) 1266
> Criminal Action No. 00-23-GMS
> September 17, 2001, Decided

Editorial Information: Subsequent History

Motion denied by United States v. Trala, 2002 U.S. Dist. LEXIS 21624 (D. Del., Nov. 8, 2002)Affirmed by United States v. Trala, 2004 U.S. App. LEXIS 22264 (3d Cir. Del., Oct. 26, 2004)

Disposition:
> Motion to Exclude Expert Testimony on DNA Analysis (D.I. 74) filed by defendant, John Walter Trala DENIED.

Counsel    For United States of America, Plaintiff: Colm F. Connelly, United States Attorney, Keith M. Rosen, Assistant United States Attorney, Wilmington, Delaware.
For John Walter Trala, Defendant: Penny Marshall, Assistant Federal Public Defender, Wilmington, Delaware.

Judges: Gregory M. Sleet, UNITED STATES DISTRICT JUDGE.

CASE SUMMARY [handwritten: misdirection and misquotation at 341]

PROCEDURAL POSTURE: Defendant was indicted for robbery while armed, conspiracy, and using a firearm during a crime of violence. He moved in limine to exclude the government's expected expert trial testimony on the results of the analysis of deoxyribonucleic acid (DNA) evidence found near the crime scene. The court conducted a Daubert hearing. In an armed robbery prosecution, applying the Daubert and Downing factors for assessing the reliability of expert testimony, the court denied defendant's motion in limine to exclude testimony on the results of the analysis of DNA evidence.

OVERVIEW: The Federal Bureau of Investigation (FBI) laboratory used polymerase chain reaction (PCR)/short tandem repeats (STR) typing to analyze the DNA evidence. The laboratory used Cofiler and Profiler materials kits during that analysis. The court held that the kits were not a separate part of the typing process. Instead, they contained materials for beginning the PCR process. Applying the Daubert and Downing factors for analyzing the reliability of expert testimony, the court held that the challenged testimony was admissible. Further, many of the defendant's arguments went to the weight, not the admissibility, of the evidence. The government presented evidence that the FBI laboratory had sufficient quality control and quality assurance measures in place and that the laboratory had procedures for preventing contamination. The record did not support the argument that the FBI improperly controlled the DNA typing industry or that the influence of one of the FBI's experts caused a "lack of real checks on the FBI product." The FBI had attempted to control for laboratory error. Finally, defendant's proposed process for calculating error rates was inappropriate.

OUTCOME: The court denied defendant's motion.

## 2. Description of DNA testing

In this case, the laboratory used a method of DNA typing known as PCR/STR typing. In PCR/STR typing, a process {162 F. Supp. 2d 341} known as polymerase chain reaction, or PCR, is used to amplify targeted loci of the sample of DNA by replicating the process by which DNA duplicates itself naturally. Thus, the lab is able to produce a substantial number of specific, targeted segments of DNA which can then be typed and compared. Short Tandem Repeats, or STRs, are a group of loci which are used to type and compare the DNA. Finally, statistics are used to evaluate how likely it is that a similar match would occur if the DNA sample were drawn randomly from the population. The court will briefly further describe the typing methods used below.

### a. PCR Amplification Process 2

PCR, a sample preparation technique, is a laboratory process for copying a short segment of DNA millions of times. The PCR process is analogous to the process by which cells replicate their DNA naturally. *See United States v. Gaines*, 979 F. Supp. at 1435. By using this process, a lab can produce a substantial number of specific, targeted segments of DNA which can then be typed and compared. PCR allows the laboratory to amplify only those specific DNA regions which exhibit genetic variations within the population, allowing for DNA typing. Moreover, the PCR process enables the analysis of very tiny amounts of DNA. PCR also permits the analysis of old and/or degraded DNA samples.

The PCR process is comprised of three steps. First, the double-stranded segment of DNA is separated, or denatured, into two strands by heating. This denatured DNA strand forms a template that can allow the manufacture of a new strand that is identical to its former complimentary strand.

Next, each of the single-strand segments are hybridized with primers. Primers are short DNA segments that are designed to bind with the template at particular loci. The primers are designed to compliment a sequence just outside of a target sequence of bases.

Finally, each primer serves as a starting point for the replication of the target sequence. In this third step, a type of enzyme called a polymerase becomes active. In essence, the polymerase facilitates repeated additions of bases to the primer until a new, complimentary strand of the targeted DNA locus is created.

This process is repeated a number of times, creating an exponentially increasing number of copies of the targeted area of the original DNA. Eventually, the PCR amplification process yields a sufficient quantity of the DNA sample to be typed. If the laboratory wants to type the DNA sample at multiple sites, it can add additional primers which will bind simultaneously to their respective target sites. This process is known as multiplexing. According to Dr. Budowle, multiplexing allows the laboratory to minimize the chance of human error and contamination in the PCR process. Using current technology, the FBI laboratory can multiplex up to fifteen or sixteen markers with reliable results.

### b. Short Tandem Repeats 3

The PCR process is performed to amplify a targeted locus (or loci) for analysis. {162 F. Supp. 2d 342}

*RE MANUFACTURE*

*SEE GAINES AT 979 F Supp. 1432 for ACTUAL QUOTE*

# Exhibit 8

Description: United States v. Gaines, 979 F. Supp. 1429 at 1432 and at 1435 (U.S. District Court S.D. Florida 1997) (citing Beasley supra at 1432).

UNITED STATES OF AMERICA v. LEETAVIOUS GAINES and BOGARD LIDDELL, Defendants
UNITED STATES DISTRICT COURT FOR THE SOUTHERN DISTRICT OF FLORIDA
979 F. Supp. 1429; 1997 U.S. Dist. LEXIS 19445; 48 Fed. R. Evid. Serv. (Callaghan) 419
CASE NO. 96-6159-CR-GOLD
October 3, 1997, Decided
October 3, 1997, Filed

Disposition:
Government's motion to introduce PCR-based DNA analysis GRANTED; and Defendants' motions to exclude such analysis DENIED.

Counsel
For LEETAVIOUS M. GAINES, defendant: Howard J. Schumacher, Fort Lauderdale, FL.
For BOGARD LIDDELL, defendant: Gary Robert Fine, Gary Robert Fine, P.A., Fort Lauderdale, FL.
U. S. Attorneys: Andrea Simonton, United States Attorney's Office, Miami, FL.

Judges: ALAN S. GOLD, UNITED STATES DISTRICT JUDGE.

CASE SUMMARY

PROCEDURAL POSTURE: Defendants were charged with committing six armed robberies within a ten day period and with conspiracy to commit those robberies. Defendants challenged the government's motion to admit the results of Polymerase Chain Reaction (PCR) based testing of DNA found on certain objects seized after one of the robberies. The government established the scientific validity, and thus evidentiary reliability, of tests using PCR-based DNA analysis. The test results were admissible in criminal prosecution.

OVERVIEW: Following the robbery of a restaurant, a black bandanna was picked up by police outside the drive-thru window. Later two ski masks and a ski cap were seized. These items were sent to the FBI laboratory along with blood samples from both defendants and from the brother of one of the defendants. The tests identified one of the defendants as the source of the DNA on the bandanna. The results were inconclusive regarding the other items. The court was called upon to determine the validity, and hence the reliability, of PCR based DNA analysis. The court applied the criteria set forth in Daubert v. Merrell Dow Pharmaceuticals. It determined that the PCR method had been tested, subjected to peer review and publication, that it had an acceptable rate of error, that there were standards which controlled the technique's operation, and that it had received wide general acceptance. The court went on to apply the same analysis to the process for determining a match and the random match probability. The court held that the test results were valid and reliable.

OUTCOME: The court granted the government's motion to admit the results of PCR-based DNA analysis of the bandanna and other objects and denied defendants' motions to exclude the analysis.

{979 F. Supp. 1432} 3.3 billion base pairs. Most of the base pairs are arranged in the same sequence in all humans. (citation omitted) However, every DNA molecule has regions known as polymorphic sites where variability is found in the human population. (footnote omitted) Each possible arrangement of base pairs that occurs at a polymorphic site is referred to as an allele. Alleles can result from differences in a single base pair, differences in multiple base pairs, or differences in the number of base pairs that comprise a site.

The combination of alleles from corresponding sites on a chromosome pair is sometimes referred to as the site's genotype. (footnote and citation omitted). One allele for each single locus genotype is inherited from each parent. If both parents contribute the same type of allele, the child's genotype is considered to be homozygous. If each parent contributes a different type of allele, the child's genotype is considered to be heterozygous. To illustrate, if only two alleles for a locus are found in the population, A and a, two homozygous genotypes, AA and aa, and one heterozygous genotype, Aa, will be found in the population. Although an individual's genotype consists of either two copies of the same allele or one copy of each of two different alleles, many different alleles may be found in the population for a single locus. (citation omitted)

### B. THE PCR METHOD OF DNA ANALYSIS.

The PCR method of DNA analysis has been succinctly described in *United States v. Beasley*, 102 F.3d 1440, 1445 (8th Cir. 1996), where the Eight Circuit quoted (and adopted) Judge Doty's findings which were rendered following a *Daubert* hearing. The quoted findings provide: 3

> The PCR method [of DNA analysis] is based upon the natural DNA replication process. By utilizing the PCR method, one can produce a substantial number of specific segments of human DNA which can then be typed. Because 99 percent of the DNA molecule is the same for every individual, the DNA segments amplified for purposes of PCR DNA typing are ones which exhibit genetic variation within the population. These variations provide the basis for DNA typing.

> The PCR method recognizes that the base pairs along the DNA molecule are joined by hydrogen bonds which can be broken by heating. When exposed to heating, the two complementary strands of DNA separate or "denature." Because the bases on a DNA strand are always complementary, a denatured DNA strand forms a template that allows the manufacture of a new strand that is identical to the former complementary strand. This denatured strand is then exposed to two synthetic primers, each complementing a sequence at one end of the target sequence and which bind with their complementary sequence on the separated strands. One of a type of enzymes called polymerase can be used to attach a free nucleotides [sic] to the end of the primer. Because the nitrogenous bases of nucleotide pairs are always (reference omitted) complementary, the nucleotide that is added to the end of the primer is necessarily complementary to the nucleotide on the sample DNA strand bound to the primer. Polymerase then adds another nucleotide to the nucleotide that has just been added. The second nucleotide is necessarily complementary to the next nucleotide on the sample strand. Repeated additions for the nucleotides continue until a new strand of the targeted DNA-sequence is created. The new strand is complementary to the sample strand, and thus identical to the other denatured strand of the original DNA sample.

> The replication process can be repeated by reheating the sample to again cause denaturation and with each new cycle, the DNA replicated grows exponentially. Eventually, the amplification produces a sufficient quantity of a relatively pure sample for an {979 F. Supp. 1433

{979 F. Supp. 1435} for forensic DNA analysis. In reaching these results, both courts relied on the findings of the National Research Council of the National Academy of Sciences in its report entitled, *The Evaluation of Forensic DNA Evidence* (1996)(hereinafter "1996 NRC Report II")(Ex. 6 Government's Memorandum in Support of Admissibility). With respect to the forensic use of PCR-based test evidence, the Committee noted that it had been introduced in a substantial number of cases, and judges, with few dissenters, have held that PCR-based techniques were sufficiently reliable to establish matches between samples. 1996 NRC Report at 177-78. 5 In *Lowe*, the court quoted from that part of the 1996 NRC Report which states that PCR tests are "thoroughly sound and . . . the results are highly reproducible when appropriate quality control methods are followed." *Id.* at 417.

## D. ENUMERATION AND APPLICATION OF DAUBERT FACTORS.

*Daubert* sets forth the criteria for determining whether expert scientific evidence is admissible at trial. A district court confronted with a proffer of expert testimony must at the outset, pursuant to Fed.R.Evid. 104(a) and 702, determine whether the expert is proposing to testify about "(1) scientific knowledge that (2) will assist the trier of fact to understand or determine a fact in issue. *Daubert*, 509 U.S. at 592, 113 S. Ct. At 2796. "The trial judge must ensure that any and all scientific testimony or evidence admitted is not only relevant, but reliable." U.S. at 589, S. Ct. at 2795. Among the non-exclusive factors that a court should consider in determining whether scientific testimony is reliable are: (1) whether the expert's opinion can be or has been tested; (2) whether the theory or technique on which the opinion is based has been subjected to peer review and publication; (3) the technique's known or potential error rate; (4) the existence and maintenance of standards controlling the technique's operations; and (5) "general acceptance." *Daubert*, 509 U.S. at 593-94, 113 S. Ct. at 2796-97. No single factor is necessarily dispositive in this analysis and other factors might also warrant consideration in the appropriate case. *Daubert*, 509 U.S. at 594, 113 S. Ct. at 2797.

## E. APPLICATION OF DAUBERT FACTORS TO THE EVIDENCE

Simply stated, PCR DNA based analysis involves three components--sample processing, match determination and random match probability. Each component is considered separately below under the criteria enumerated in *Daubert*.

### I. SAMPLE PROCESSING

#### A. *The PCR Method of DNA Analysis Has Been Tested*

Under *Daubert*, the first step in determining the scientific validity of a theory or technique is whether it can be or has been tested. All the samples in the case were processed using the PCR method. All sampling was performed in accordance with the FBI Laboratory protocol. The PCR process is approximately 10 years old, and has undergone extensive testing. The process was applied first to amplify the DQA1 genetic markers analyzed in the Polymarker ("PM") test and, shortly thereafter, the D1S80 genetic marker. The underlying premise upon which PCR is based is that an amplification process can be used to make many identical copies of selected portions of the DNA molecule, i.e., genetic markers, and that the resulting product can be used to determine the existence of particular types of alleles of those genetic markers.

Based on the expert testimony, the Court finds that the PCR method of analysis for these genetic markers had been tested extensively, and, when the FBI Protocol is followed, the analysis consistently generates true results. The validation studies contained in Government Exhibits 120, 121 and {979 F. Supp. 1436}

# Exhibit 9

Description: Promega v. Life Techs Corp., 2011 U.S. Dist. Lexis 158561 at 31-35 and at 41 (W.D. Wis Nov 29 2011) Amp FISTR COfiler, Profiler, Identifiler, Yfiler PCR amplification kits "NOT licensed for HUMAN LINKAGE of unknown individuals." @ Lexis 31, 34, 41

**PROMEGA CORPORATION, Plaintiff, and MAX-PLANCK-GESELLSCHAFT zur FORDERUNG der WISSENSCHAFTEN E.V., Involuntary Plaintiff, v. LIFE TECHNOLOGIES CORPORATION, INVITROGEN IP HOLDINGS, INC. and APPLIED BIOSYSTEMS, LLC, Defendants.**
**UNITED STATES DISTRICT COURT FOR THE WESTERN DISTRICT OF WISCONSIN**
**2011 U.S. Dist. LEXIS 158561**
**10-cv-281-bbc**
**November 29, 2011, Decided**
**November 29, 2011, Filed**

**Editorial Information: Subsequent History**

Later proceeding at Promega Corp. v. Life Techs. Corp., 2012 U.S. Dist. LEXIS 11206 (W.D. Wis., Jan. 31, 2012)

**Editorial Information: Prior History**

Promega Corp. v. Life Techs. Corp., 2011 U.S. App. LEXIS 20460 (Fed. Cir., Oct. 6, 2011)

**Counsel** {2011 U.S. Dist. LEXIS 1}For Promega Corporation, a Wisconsin corporation, Plaintiff: James R. Troupis, LEAD ATTORNEY, Troupis Law Office LLC, Middleton, WI; Stewart W. Karge, LEAD ATTORNEY, Karge & Associates, Chicago, IL; Brandon Michael Lewis, Troupis Law Office, Middleton, WI; Mark C. Fleming, Wilmer Cutler Pickering Hale & Dorr LLP, Boston, MA; Peter Carroll, Sarah E. Troupis Ferguson, Medlen & Carroll, LLC, Braintree, MA; Seth P. Waxman, WilmerHale, Washington, DC; Thomas G. Saunders, Wilmer Cutler Pickering Hale and Dorr LLP, Washington, DC.

Max-Planck-Gesellschaft zur Forderung der Wissenschaften E.V., involuntary plaintiff, Plaintiff, Pro se.

For Max-Planck-Gesellschaft zur Forderung der Wissenschaften E.V., involuntary plaintiff, Plaintiff: James R. Troupis, LEAD ATTORNEY, Troupis Law Office LLC, Middleton, WI.

For Life Technologies Corporation, a Delaware corporation, Defendant: Francis M. Wikstrom, Michael R. McCarthy, LEAD ATTORNEYS, Parsons Behle Latimer, Salt Lake City, UT; Steven M. Streck, LEAD ATTORNEY, Andrew J. Clarkowski, Michael J. Modl, Axley Brynelson, LLP, Madison, WI; Amy Sun, PRO HAC VICE, Life Technologies Corporation, Carlsbad, CA; Carter Glasgow Phillips, Sidley Austin LLP, Washington,{2011 U.S. Dist. LEXIS 2} DC; Edward Robert Reines, Timothy Chen Saulsbury, Weil, Gotshal & Manges LLP, Redwood Shores, CA; Jonathan Andrew Muenkel, Life Technologies Corporation, Carlsbad, CA; Katherine M. Nolan-Stevaux, Life Technologies Corporation, Foster City, CA; Kristine E. Johnson, PRO HAC VICE, Parsons Behle Latimer, Salt Lake City, UT.

For Applied Biosystems, LLC, Defendant: Francis M. Wikstrom, LEAD ATTORNEY, Michael R. McCarthy, Parsons Behle Latimer, Salt Lake City, UT; Amy Sun, PRO HAC VICE, Life Technologies Corporation, Carlsbad, CA; Carter Glasgow Phillips, Sidley Austin LLP, Washington, DC; Edward Robert Reines, Timothy Chen Saulsbury, Weil, Gotshal & Manges LLP, Redwood Shores, CA; Jonathan Andrew Muenkel, Life Technologies Corporation, Carlsbad, CA; Katherine M. Nolan-Stevaux, Life Technologies Corporation, Foster City, CA; Kristine E. Johnson, PRO HAC VICE, Parsons Behle Latimer, Salt Lake City, UT.

For Invitrogen IP Holdings, Inc., Defendant: Francis M. Wikstrom,

LEAD ATTORNEY, Michael R. McCarthy, Parsons Behle Latimer, Salt Lake City, UT; Amy Sun, PRO HAC VICE, Life Technologies Corporation, Carlsbad, CA; Andrew J. Clarkowski, Axley Brynelson, LLP, Madison, WI; Edward Robert Reines, Timothy {2011 U.S. Dist. LEXIS 3} Chen Saulsbury, Weil, Gotshal & Manges LLP, Redwood Shores, CA; Jonathan Andrew Muenkel, Life Technologies Corporation, Carlsbad, CA; Katherine M. Nolan-Stevaux, Life Technologies Corporation, Foster City, CA; Kristine E. Johnson, PRO HAC VICE, Parsons Behle Latimer, Salt Lake City, UT.

For Invitrogen IP Holdings, Inc., Counter Claimant: Amy Sun, PRO HAC VICE, Life Technologies Corporation, Carlsbad, CA; Andrew J. Clarkowski, Axley Brynelson, LLP, Madison, WI; Carter Glasgow Phillips, Sidley Austin LLP, Washington, DC; Edward Robert Reines, Timothy Chen Saulsbury, Weil, Gotshal & Manges LLP, Redwood Shores, CA; Jonathan Andrew Muenkel, Life Technologies Corporation, Carlsbad, CA; Katherine M. Nolan-Stevaux, Life Technologies Corporation, Foster City, CA; Kristine E. Johnson, PRO HAC VICE, Parsons Behle Latimer, Salt Lake City, UT; Michael R. McCarthy, Parsons Behle Latimer, Salt Lake City, UT.

For Applied Biosystems, LLC, Counter Claimant: Amy Sun, PRO HAC VICE, Life Technologies Corporation, Carlsbad, CA; Edward Robert Reines, Timothy Chen Saulsbury, Weil, Gotshal & Manges LLP, Redwood Shores, CA; Jonathan Andrew Muenkel, Life Technologies Corporation, Carlsbad, CA; Katherine M. Nolan-Stevaux,{2011 U.S. Dist. LEXIS 4} Life Technologies Corporation, Foster City, CA; Kristine E. Johnson, PRO HAC VICE, Parsons Behle Latimer, Salt Lake City, UT; Michael R. McCarthy, Parsons Behle Latimer, Salt Lake City, UT.

For Life Technologies Corporation, a Delaware corporation, Counter Claimant: Francis M. Wikstrom, Michael R. McCarthy, LEAD ATTORNEYS, Parsons Behle Latimer, Salt Lake City, UT; Steven M. Streck, LEAD ATTORNEY, Andrew J. Clarkowski, Michael J. Modl, Axley Brynelson, LLP, Madison, WI; Amy Sun, PRO HAC VICE, Life Technologies Corporation, Carlsbad, CA; Edward Robert Reines, Timothy Chen Saulsbury, Weil, Gotshal & Manges LLP, Redwood Shores, CA; Jonathan Andrew Muenkel, Life Technologies Corporation, Carlsbad, CA; Katherine M. Nolan-Stevaux, Life Technologies Corporation, Foster City, CA; Kristine E. Johnson, PRO HAC VICE, Parsons Behle Latimer, Salt Lake City, UT.

For Promega Corporation, a Wisconsin corporation, Counter Defendant: James R. Troupis, LEAD ATTORNEY, Troupis Law Office LLC, Middleton, WI; Stewart W. Karge, LEAD ATTORNEY, Karge & Associates, Chicago, IL; Brandon Michael Lewis, Troupis Law Office, Middleton, WI; Peter Carroll, Sarah E. Troupis Ferguson, Medlen & Carroll, LLC, Braintree,{2011 U.S. Dist. LEXIS 5} MA; Susan Rebecca Podolsky, Alexandria, VA.

**Judges:** BARBARA B. CRABB, District Judge.

## Opinion

**Opinion by:** BARBARA B. CRABB

## Opinion

### OPINION AND ORDER

Plaintiff Promega Corporation is suing defendants Life Technologies Corporation, Applied Biosystems,

LLC and Invitrogen IP Holdings, Inc. for infringement of U.S. Patents Nos. 5,843,660, 6,221,598, 6,479,235, 7,008,771 and Re 37,984. (Both sides treat the three defendants as one entity for the purpose of the motions for summary judgment, so I will do the same.) Plaintiff owns the first four patents and is the exclusive licensee of involuntary plaintiff Max Planck with respect to the fifth. The patents relate to "multiplex amplification of short tandem repeat loci," which are regions on a DNA strand that contain repeating nucleotide sequences. Because the number of repeats of particular sequences can vary greatly from person to person, these differences can be used to compare different DNA samples for possible matches. To facilitate the process, the loci are copied, or "amplified." "Multiplex" amplification means that multiple loci are copied simultaneously to make the process more efficient.

The asserted patents include both apparatus and method claims. Plaintiff contends that kits made and sold by defendants directly infringe the {2011 U.S. Dist. LEXIS 6} apparatus claims and that defendants induce infringement of the method claims. The asserted apparatus claims are claims 18-19 and 21-23 of the '235 patent, claims 10, 23-24, 27 and 33 of the '598 patent; claims 25 and 27-31 of the '660 patent, claim 5 of the '771 patent and claim 42 of the '984 patent. The asserted method claims are claims 1-4, 6-13 and 15-17 of the '235 patent, claims 1-2, 4-5, 7-9, 12, 15, 19, 21-22, 28 and 31-32 of the '598 patent; claims 2-5, 16-17, 19-21 and 23-24 of the '660 patent and claims 15-16, 18, 23, 25, 27-28 and 41 of the '984 patent.

Plaintiff has filed a motion for summary judgment with respect to infringement of all five patents as well as on defendants' invalidity defenses and counterclaims for anticipation, lack of enablement and obviousness. Defendants have filed a motion for partial summary judgment for noninfringement, lack of enablement and obviousness with respect to all of the patents except the '984 patent.

I am granting defendants' motion with respect to noninfringement of claims 25 and 27-31 of the '660 patent because I conclude that those claims are limited to products that use no loci other than those listed in the claims and the parties agree that none of the accused products are limited to just those loci. Because the remaining asserted claims are open-ended {2011 U.S. Dist. LEXIS 7} (they do not exclude unrecited loci) and the parties identify no other potential differences between the accused products, I am granting plaintiff's motion for summary judgment with respect to direct infringement of all other claims that disclose a kit. I disagree with defendants that their sale of the kits is covered by a license agreement with plaintiff and that plaintiff lacks standing to sue under the '984 patent.

With respect to the method claims, plaintiff is not seeking summary judgment for direct infringement, only for inducement under 35 U.S.C. § 271(b). I am denying plaintiff's motion for summary judgment with respect to inducement and willfulness because plaintiff failed to develop arguments on these issues. Because defendants' motion for summary judgment did not include these issues, they will have to proceed to trial.

With respect to invalidity, I conclude that plaintiff is entitled to summary judgment on defendants' affirmative defenses and counterclaims of anticipation, obviousness and lack of enablement. The enablement defense is contingent on an incorrect view that the patentees were required to enable unrecited elements and defendants have failed to adduce any evidence that at the time the patent {2011 U.S. Dist. LEXIS 8} applications were filed, it would have been obvious to a person of ordinary skill in the art that the combinations of loci disclosed in the asserted patents could coamplify successfully.

Defendants do not contend in their summary judgment briefs that any of the claims in the asserted patents are anticipated, but they say that the court should not rule on this issue because they never raised it. I disagree. Although it is true that defendants did not include an opinion on anticipation in their expert report, in their answer they included an affirmative defense and a counterclaim that "the

'660, '598, '235, and '771 patents are invalid for failure to comply with one or more of the requirements of the United States patent laws, including at least 35 U.S.C. sections 102, 103 and/or 112." Ans., dkt. #150, at 35. Anticipation is one of the defenses under 35 U.S.C. § 102. Defendants did not explicitly identify anticipation as a defense or a counterclaim, but they did not identify any other particular invalidity defenses either. Thus, if defendants properly raised any invalidity defenses in their answer and counterclaim, anticipation was among them. Accordingly, I conclude that there is an actual controversy regarding that issue and that plaintiff is entitled{2011 U.S. Dist. LEXIS 9} to summary judgment because defendants failed to show that a genuine issue of material fact exists.

Two other motions are before the court: (1) plaintiff's motion to "strike" defendants' brief in support of their motion for partial summary judgment, or, in the alternative, to disregard any facts not included in defendants' proposed findings of fact, dkt. #262; and (2) plaintiff's motion for leave to file a reply brief in support of the motion to strike. Dkt. #293. With respect to the motion to strike, I will grant plaintiff's alternative request because the court's procedures are clear that "[a]ll facts necessary to sustain a party's position on a motion for summary judgment must be explicitly proposed as findings of fact." Helpful Tips for Filing a Summary Judgment Motion, Tip #1, dkt. #69, at 11. See also Procedure to Be Followed on Motions for Summary Judgment, I.B.4, dkt, #69, at 14 ("The court will not consider facts contained only in a brief."). I have not considered facts submitted by either side unless they were included in its proposed findings of fact. Plaintiff's motion to file a reply brief will be denied as unnecessary.

BACKGROUND

Certain locations or "loci" on chromosomes vary{2011 U.S. Dist. LEXIS 10} from individual to individual. These are called polymorphic loci and are useful as identifiers. However, no one locus will positively identify an individual to a statistically significant degree because no one locus is unique to each individual within any given population.

Short tandem repeats (STRs) are loci found within genomic DNA that have a number of short repetitive nucleotide sequences. The DNA sequences at a particular STR locus within a given population will exhibit a variable number of these repeat sequences. It is this variation in the number of repeats at a particular locus that is responsible for the polymorphisms that permit scientists to genetically distinguish one individual from another.

Polymerase chain reaction is one method of amplifying loci. There are several steps in the process. First, the two strands of genomic DNA are heated and then separated to form "single stranded" DNA. Second, a pair of "primers" is introduced and allowed to pair with the single stranded DNA. This pairing occurs in accordance with the nucleotide pairing rules, that is, at a point on the single stranded DNA where the primer sequence is complementary to the genomic nucleotide sequence.

Amplifying{2011 U.S. Dist. LEXIS 11} the alleles present at a single locus is commonly referred to as a "monoplex" reaction. Amplifying multiple STR loci simultaneously is a "multiplex" reaction. To minimize labor, materials and analysis time, it is desirable to analyze multiple loci and samples simultaneously. One approach for reaching this goal involves amplification of multiple loci simultaneously in a single reaction.

The amplified alleles from one DNA sample can be compared to the amplified alleles of a second DNA sample by, for example, running the two samples side-by-side on the gel. One can then determine whether the two samples came from the same individual. Additionally, a "size marker" or "allelic ladder" is often run concurrently with the sample in another lane of the gel. By comparing the alleles amplified in the DNA sample to the allelic ladder one can determine precisely which alleles appear in the DNA sample.

Defendants manufacture, offer for sale and sell AmpFlSTR Amplification Kits. These kits provide components for carrying out simultaneous amplification of multiple short tandem repeat loci from one or more DNA samples. The kits are used for chimerism in the context of bone marrow transplant monitoring, {2011 U.S. Dist. LEXIS 12} cell line authentication, genotyping hydatidiform moles, cancer analysis, determinations of fetal sex and anthropological research, among other things.

Chimerism occurs following bone marrow transplantation when the recipient produces her own blood cells as well as donor blood cells. The kits are used to compare the amount of amplified STR alleles from the donor and host and then to determine the proportion of blood cells contributed by each source. Repetitive testing over time indicates whether the proportion of blood cells from the donor and host is changing, which has treatment and prognostic value.

In genotyping hydatidiform moles, kits are used to classify moles in a woman's uterus during pregnancy to assess whether the woman is at risk for particular diseases. In cell line authentication, kits are used to determine whether new cell lines are unique. In cancer analysis, the kits are used to analyze genetic instability in cancers by detecting allelic imbalance.

OPINION

A. Claim Construction

The parties' arguments on questions of infringement and invalidity rely in part on their understanding of the phrase "a set of . . . loci," which appears in all of the asserted claims in the '235, '598, {2011 U.S. Dist. LEXIS 13} '660, and '771 patents. In particular, each claim includes the phrase "a set of . . . loci" followed by a list of particular loci. For example, claim 16 of the '660 patent discloses:

> A method of simultaneously determining the alleles present in three short tandem repeat loci from one or more DNA samples, comprising:
>
> (a) obtaining at least one DNA sample to be analyzed,
>
> (b) selecting a set of three short tandem repeat loci of the DNA sample to be analyzed which can be amplified together, wherein the set of three loci is selected from the group of sets of loci consisting of:
>
> D3S1539, D19S253, D13S317;
>
> D10S1239, D9S930, D20S481;
>
> D10S1239, D4S2368, D20S481;
>
> D10S1239, D9S930, D4S2368;
>
> D16S539, D7S820, D13S317; and
>
> D10S1239, D9S930, D13S317.
>
> (c) co-amplifying the three loci in the set in a multiplex amplification reaction, wherein the product of the reaction is a mixture of amplified alleles from each of the co-amplified loci in the set; and
>
> (d) evaluating the amplified alleles in the mixture to determine the alleles present at each of the loci analyzed in the set within the DNA sample. The question of claim construction presented by the parties is whether the set may include loci in addition to those that are listed in the claim, {2011 U.S. Dist. LEXIS 14} that is, whether the set is open or closed. Plaintiff says all of the asserted claims are open-ended; defendants say they are all closed.

The parties raised this issue in their claim construction briefs, but I declined to resolve it because both sides supported their arguments with text of particular claims without accounting for the textual differences among the claims. Accordingly, I directed the parties to reassert their arguments at summary judgment if they believed a construction was needed to resolve a dispute of infringement or invalidity. "In the meantime, the parties should consider how they wish to frame their arguments. If they believe that 'a set of . . . loci' has an identical meaning everywhere it appears in every asserted claim in every asserted patent, then they should be prepared to explain why textual differences in the claims may be disregarded. They should not use the language of a particular claim to support a construction they wish to be applied across the board." Dkt. #190, at 4.

Defendants largely disregarded these instructions in their summary judgment materials. They advance arguments from the prosecution history with the assumption that a statement from the{2011 U.S. Dist. LEXIS 15} history of one patent applies equally to another and they cherry pick language from particular claims while ignoring other claims that have different texts.

I will consider defendants' arguments about the prosecution history first and I will assume that any statement in the prosecution history applies to all of the asserted patents. Defendants argue that the applicants disclaimed the inclusion of any loci in the reaction not expressly listed in the claims. In support, defendants cite various statements from the applicants that the prior art did not include "these combinations" of loci and a statement from the examiner of the '598 patent that the prior art "does not teach the specific combinations provided in the claims." Dfts.' Br., dkt. #245, at 12-13. (Defendants did not include proposed findings of fact about these aspects of the prosecution history, but I will consider them because doing so will not make any difference to the outcome of the motion.)

If the applicants had been distinguishing prior art that included one of the listed sets of loci *and* one or more additional loci, defendants would have a stronger argument of disclaimer. Defendants' argument fails because the applicants were distinguishing{2011 U.S. Dist. LEXIS 16} prior art that was *missing* some of the loci in the listed combinations. For example, the applicants noted that Oldroyd included two of the loci listed in claim 1 of '660 patent, but none of the other loci. Dkt. #240-12. Thus, a statement that "these combinations" were not in the prior art does not disclaim an invention that includes those combinations and additional loci.

The cases defendants cite provide no support for their argument. In Seachange International, Inc. v. C-COR, Inc., 413 F.3d 1361, 1369 (Fed. Cir. 2005), the question was whether the applicants had defined the term "network for data communications" to mean "point-to-point networks" during the prosecution history. In concluding that they had, the court of appeals relied on statements in which the applicants overcame an examiner's objection by explaining that the prior art did not include a point-to-point network. In Elkay Manufacturing Co. v. Ebco Manufacturing Co., 192 F.3d 973, 977 (Fed. Cir. 1999), the question was whether the term "an upstanding feed tube" meant one tube or could mean more than one. The court limited the term to one tube because, during the prosecution history, the applicants had distinguished prior art on the ground that it used multiple tubes.

Neither of these cases raised the question whether the claimed invention is limited to recited items. Both involved applicants who{2011 U.S. Dist. LEXIS 17} needed to narrowly define their invention during prosecution in order to overcome an anticipation defense. Because the applicants in this case did not define their invention to exclude additional loci, SeaChange and Elkay are not on point.

Defendants' other "universal" argument is similar. They rely on Smith v. Snow, 294 U.S. 1, 14, 55 S. Ct. 279, 79 L. Ed. 721, 1935 Dec. Comm'r Pat. 757 (1935), Phillips v. AWH Corp., 415 F.3d 1303, 1321 (Fed. Cir. 2005), Acumed, LLC v. Stryker Corp., 483 F.3d 800, 815 (Fed. Cir. 2007), and In re Gray, 53 F.2d 520, 522, 19 C.C.P.A. 745, 1932 Dec. Comm'r Pat. 85 (CCPA 1931), for the proposition that claims should not be construed to cover more than what was actually invented. Because the applicants did not invent any combinations of loci other than those listed in the claims, defendants say it would violate this principle to allow the claims to cover additional loci.

Again, none of the cited cases raise the question whether a claim must be limited to recited elements. It is well-established that claims are not so limited; that is the whole point of using terms such as "comprising" or "including." Crystal Semiconductor Corp. v. TriTech Microelectronics International, Inc., 246 F.3d 1336, 1348 (Fed Cir. 2001) ("[T]he transition 'comprising' creates a presumption that the recited elements are only a part of the device, that the claim does not exclude additional, unrecited elements."); AFG Industries, Inc. v. Cardinal IG Co., Inc., 239 F.3d 1239, 1244 (Fed. Cir. 2001) ("When a claim uses an 'open' transition phrase, its scope may cover devices that employ additional, unrecited elements."); Stiftung v. Renishaw PLC, 945 F.2d 1173, 1178 (Fed. Cir. 1991) (a claim that "uses the term 'comprising,' is an 'open'{2011 U.S. Dist. LEXIS 18} claim which will read on devices which add additional elements"). If I were to accept defendants' argument, it would mean that a defendant could avoid infringement simply by adding more elements to a device or method. That is not the law, even when the additional elements are an improvement to the claimed invention. Free Motion Fitness, Inc. v. Cybex International, Inc., 423 F.3d 1343, 1347 (Fed. Cir. 2005) ("The addition of unclaimed elements does not typically defeat infringement when a patent uses an open transitional phrase such as 'comprising.'"); Lighting World, Inc. v. Birchwood Lighting, Inc., 382 F.3d 1354, 1365 (Fed. Cir. 2004) ("Making improvements on a patented invention by adding features to a claimed device beyond those recited in the patent does not avoid infringement."); A.B. Dick Co. v. Burroughs Corp., 713 F.2d 700, 703 (Fed. Cir. 1983) ("It is fundamental that one cannot avoid infringement merely by adding elements if each element recited in the claims is found in the accused device."). See also Gillette Co. v. Energizer Holdings, Inc., 405 F.3d 1367, 1374 (Fed. Cir. 2005) (claim disclosing razor with three blades could read on razor with four blades); Genentech, Inc. v. Chiron Corp., 112 F.3d 495, 499 (Fed. Cir. 1997) ("[T]he district court improperly limited the transitional phrase 'comprising,' which allows additional elements to be present as long as the named elements are present, to exclude additional DNA between the alpha-factor processing sequences and the human IGF-I sequence.").

Turning to the language of the asserted claims, I will begin with{2011 U.S. Dist. LEXIS 19} the '660 patent because I construed some of those claims in a previous case. Promega Corporation v. Applera Corporation, No. 01-C-244-C (W.D. Wis. June 10, 2002), dkt. #64. The question in case no. 01-C-244-C was the same as in this case, whether "a set of . . . loci" in the asserted claims was opened or closed. In this case, plaintiff is asserting claims 2-5, 16-17, 19-21, 23-25 and 27-31; in case no. 01-C-244-C, plaintiff was asserting claims 1-5 and 16. Although claim 1 is not asserted in this case, it is relevant because claims 2-5 depend from it. Claim 1 discloses:

> A method of simultaneously determining the alleles present in at least four short tandem repeat loci from one or more DNA samples, comprising:
>
> (a) obtaining at least one DNA sample to be analyzed,
>
> (b) selecting a set of at least four short tandem repeat loci of the DNA sample to be analyzed which can be amplified together, wherein the at least four loci in the set are selected from the group of loci consisting of:
>
> D3S1539, D4S2368, D5S818, D7S820, D9S930, D10S1239, D13S317,
>
> D14S118, D14S548, D14S562, D16S490, D16S539, D16S753, D17S1298,
>
> D17S1299, D19S253, D20S481, D22S683, HUMCSF1PO, HUMTPOX,
>
> HUMTH01, HUMF13A01, HUMBFXIII, HUMLIPOL,{2011 U.S. Dist. LEXIS 20} HUMvWFA31;
>
> (c) co-amplifying the loci in the set in a multiplex amplification reaction, wherein the product of the

reaction is a mixture of amplified alleles from each of the co-amplified loci in the set; and

(d) evaluating the amplified alleles in the mixture to determine the alleles present at each of the loci analyzed in the set within the DNA sample.

A review of the 2002 opinion reveals that there were *two* disputes about the scope of the claims, both of which seem to be relevant to this case. The first was the one focused on by the parties in this case, that is, whether the list of loci in step (b) is exclusive or may include other unnamed loci. The second was whether step (c) may include loci not listed in step (b), regardless whether the list in step (b) is closed. Both sides raise arguments about both issues, though neither acknowledges that the issues are distinct. In any event, the parties seem to agree that the accused products infringe the claims of the '660 patent if plaintiff prevails on either issue.

In case no. 01-C-244-C, I agreed initially with the defendants that lists of loci identified in claims 1-5 and 16 were closed and that the loci in step (c) were limited to the list in step{**2011 U.S. Dist. LEXIS 21**} (b). Promega Corporation v. Applera Corporation, No. 01-C-244-C, 2002 U.S. Dist. LEXIS 26927 (W.D. Wis. Jan. 2, 2002), dkt. #40. However, upon reconsideration, I adopted the following construction: "Claims 1 through 5 and 16 of the '660 Patent require the presence of at least one of the sets identified in the Markush groups stated in limitation (b) of those claims but do not exclude the presence of other STR loci in the multiplex reaction required by limitation (c) of those claims." Dkt. #64, at 10. In reaching that conclusion, I discussed several factors.

First, I concluded that it was important not to conflate the loci in "the set" in step (b) with the loci in the "reaction" in step (c). That is, even if "the set" in step (b) was limited to the recited loci, it did not follow that the loci in the "multiplex amplification reaction" in step (c) was limited to those listed in step (b). I concluded that the language of step (c) did not exclude the presence of other loci. (Plaintiff buttresses that conclusion in this case by pointing out that step (c) discloses a "mixture," which generally permits ingredients not listed in the claim. Mars, Inc. v. H.J. Heinz Co., 377 F.3d 1369 (Fed. Cir. 2004).)

Second, I cited the rule that "[o]ne who does not infringe an independent claim cannot infringe{**2011 U.S. Dist. LEXIS 22**} a claim dependent on (and thus containing all the limitations of) that claim." Wahpeton Canvas Co., Inc. v. Frontier, Inc., 870 F.2d 1546, 1552 (Fed. Cir. 1989). Under the defendants' view, this rule would be broken because it would be possible for an accused product to infringe a dependent claim without infringing the independent claim. For example, claim 3 contains the following set of loci: "D16S539, D7S820, D13S317, D5S818, HUMFI3A01, HUMFESFPS." Although the first five of these loci are listed in claim 1, HUMFESFPS is not. Thus, if the set of loci in claim 1 is closed, a product that included the six loci in claim 3 could infringe claim 3, but not claim 1.

Third, I rejected the defendants' argument that the patentees disclaimed an open set when they amended the phrase "at least four of the loci in the set" to "the at least four loci in the set." Although I acknowledged the possibility that inclusion of "the" could be read "to require that all the loci in a set, whether four or more, be selected from the Markush group in step (b)," I also found credible plaintiff's argument that "the amendment was not substantive, but was made instead to conform the claim to standard patent claim drafting procedure, which requires that an element of a claim be preceded by a{**2011 U.S. Dist. LEXIS 23**} definite article, such as 'the,' each time it is referred to after its initial appearance in a claim." Dkt. #64, at 8-9. Because neither the patentees nor the examiner made a clear statement regarding the amendment's significance, I declined to narrow the scope of the claim.

Finally, I cited a statement by the patentees when they deleted the HUMFESFPS loci from the list in claim 1: "the amendments to claim 1 do not change the fact that the claimed method encompasses the coamplification and evaluation of sets of short tandem repeat loci which include the deleted locus, provided at least four of the loci in the set . . . are selected from the remaining group of loci listed in claim 1." Because there was no clear evidence that the patentees ever disavowed this broad interpretation or that the examiner disagreed with it, the statement supported plaintiff's view that the set was open.

As I noted in the claim construction order in this case, the law suggests that I am not bound by the conclusion in the 2002 opinion because the case settled before judgment. Talmage v. Harris, 486 F.3d 968, 974 (7th Cir. 2007) ("Normally, when a case is resolved by settlement or stipulation, courts will find that the 'valid final judgment' requirement of issue{2011 U.S. Dist. LEXIS 24} preclusion has not been satisfied."). However, defendants do not directly address the 2002 opinion or criticize its reasoning. Although they raise arguments that would conflict with the earlier case, those arguments are undeveloped and unpersuasive. Accordingly, I decline to depart from my previous conclusion.

This resolves the claim construction dispute with respect to claims 2-5 and 16 of the '660 patent. Because asserted claims 17, 19-21 and 23-24 all depend from claim 16 and do not include any additional "set of . . . loci" limitations, I need not consider those claims separately.

Claims 1-2, 4-5 and 7-9 of the '598 patent have a structure similar to that of claims 2-5 and 16 of the '660 patent. Because defendants do not point to any more restrictive language in claims 1-2, 4-5 and 7-9 of the '598 patent, I conclude that those claims may include unrecited loci as well.

Asserted claim 25 in the '660 patent is another matter. That claim discloses:

> A kit for simultaneously analyzing short tandem repeat sequences in at least three loci, comprising a container which has oligonucleotide primers for co-amplifying a set of at least three short tandem repeat loci, wherein the set of loci are selected from the sets of loci consisting of:
>
> D3S1539,{2011 U.S. Dist. LEXIS 25} D19S253, D13S317;
>
> D10S1239, D9S930, D20S481;
>
> D10S1239, D4S2368, D20S481;
>
> D10S1239, D9S930, D4S2368;
>
> D16S539, D7S820, D13S317;
>
> D10S1239, D9S930, D13S317;
>
> D3S1539, D7S820, D13S317, D5S818;
>
> D17S1298, D7S820, D13S317, D5S818;
>
> D20S481, D7S820, D13S317, D5S818;
>
> D9S930, D7S820, D13S317, D5S818;
>
> D10S1239, D7S820, D13S317, D5S818;
>
> D14S118, D7S820, D13S317, D5S818;
>
> D14S562, D7S820, D13S317, D5S818;
>
> D14S548, D7S820, D13S317, D5S818;
>
> D16S490, D7S820, D13S317, D5S818;
>
> D17S1299, D7S820, D13S317, D5S818;
>
> D16S539, D7S820, D13S317, D5S818;

D22S683, D7S820, D13S317, D5S818;

D16S753, D7S820, D13S317, D5S818;

D3S1539, D19S253, D13S317, D20S481;

D3S1539, D19S253, D4S2368, D20S481;

D10S1239, D9S930, D4S2368, D20S481;

D16S539, D7S820, D13S317, HUMvWFA31;

D16S539, D7S820, D13S317, D5S818, HUMCSF1PO, HUMTPOX;

D16S539, D7S820, D13S317, D5S818, HUMF13A01, HUMFESFPS;

D16S539, D7S820, D13S317, D5S818, HUMCSF1PO, HUMTPOX, HUMTH01;

D16S539, D7S820, D13S317, D5S818, HUMF13A01, HUMFESFPS, HUMBFXIII;

D16S539, D7S820, D13S317, D5S818, HUMCSF1PO, HUMTPOX, HUMTH01, HUMvWFA31; and

D16S539, D7S820, D13S317, D5S818, HUMF13A01, HUMFESFPS, HUMBFXIII, HUMLIPOL.

Both sides recognize that the phrase "consisting of" signals a closed list. "In simple terms,{2011 U.S. Dist. LEXIS 26} a drafter uses the phrase 'consisting of' to mean 'I claim what follows and nothing else.'" Vehicular Technologies Corp. v. Titan Wheel Intern., Inc., 212 F.3d 1377, 1383 (Fed. Cir. 2000). Extending that logic to this claim would mean that the set must include loci from the list and no other loci. Unlike claims 2-5 and 16, claim 25 does not include a counterpart to step (c) that would allow unrecited loci to be included in a mixture. In addition, no claims depend from claim 25 that recite loci not included in claim 25.

Plaintiff asks the court not to construe claim 25 as closed because the claim includes the term "comprising," which it says supports a construction that additional, unrecited loci may be included. Although plaintiff is correct that the term "comprising" is open-ended, as defendants point out, the term "'[c]omprising' is not a weasel word with which to abrogate claim limitations." Spectrum International Inc. v. Sterilite Corp., 164 F.3d 1372, 1380 (Fed. Cir. 1998). The context of the term is important. In claim 25, "'[c]omprising' appears at the beginning of the claim . . . The presumption raised by the term 'comprising' does not reach into each of the [elements] to render every word and phrase therein open-ended." Dippin' Dots, Inc. v. Mosey. 476 F.3d 1337, 1343 (Fed. Cir. 2007). In other words, the term "comprising" in claim 25 suggests that the kit may include elements other than "a container which has oligonucleotide primers for{2011 U.S. Dist. LEXIS 27} co-amplifying a set of at least three short tandem repeat loci," but it does not suggest that the set may include loci outside the list.

The importance of context is shown by comparison to asserted claim 10 of the '598 patent:

> A kit for simultaneously analyzing short tandem repeat sequences in at least three loci, comprising:
>
> a single container containing oligonucleotide primers for each locus in a set of at least three short tandem repeat loci, wherein the at least three short tandem repeat loci in the set comprises at least three loci selected from the group consisting of: [a listing of 20 sets of three loci].

In this claim, the applicants wrote that the set "comprises at least three loci selected from the" recited group, making it clear that the set may include other loci outside the group. Claim 25 of the '660 patent is missing similar language.

Alternatively, plaintiff relies on the phrase "at least three loci" in claim 25: "the fact that the sets themselves (from which to choose) are bigger than three loci makes it expressly clear additional loci can be selected." Plt.'s Br., dkt. #228, at 11. This argument makes no sense. If the listed sets were limited to two or three loci, then the phrase "at least{2011 U.S. Dist. LEXIS 28} three loci" might support an argument that additional loci must be present as well. However, because some of the listed sets have three loci and some have more than three, there is no reason to interpret "at least three loci" as anything other than an acknowledgment that some of the listed sets have more than three loci in them.

Accordingly, I conclude that claim 25 of the '660 patent is limited to the listed loci. Because asserted claims 27-31 depend from claim 25, this conclusion extends to those claims as well.

The language of the remaining asserted independent claims makes it clear that they are not limited to the recited loci because they all use the word "comprising" when listing the loci. '598 pat., claim 12 ("selecting a set of short tandem repeat loci of the DNA sample to be analyzed which can be co-amplified, comprising . . ."); id. at claim 23 ("a set of short tandem repeat loci which can be co-amplified, comprising . . ."); id. at claim 28 ("a set of short tandem repeat loci of the DNA sample to be analyzed which can be co-amplified, comprising . . . "); id. at claim 33 ("a set of short tandem repeat loci which can be co-amplified, comprising . . . "); '235 pat., claim 1 ("selecting{2011 U.S. Dist. LEXIS 29} a set of loci of the DNA sample, comprising . . ."); id. at claim 13 ("selecting a set of loci of the DNA sample, comprising . . ."); id. at claim 18 ("the loci comprise . . ."); '771 pat., claim 5 ("a set of loci from one or more DNA samples, comprising . . ."). The remaining asserted claims of these four patents are dependent claims that do not include more limiting language that is relevant to this issue. Accordingly, I conclude that all of the asserted claims allow for unrecited loci, with the exception of claims 25 and 27-31 of the '660 patent.

B. Infringement

Plaintiff contends that summary judgment is appropriate for direct infringement with respect to those asserted claims that disclose a kit and inducement of infringement with respect to the method claims. Defendants do not deny in their briefs that the accused products include all of the elements of the '984 patent. With respect to the '660, '598, '235 and '771 patents, the only element defendants say is missing is "a set of . . . loci" on the ground that the accused products include loci not recited in the claims. In the previous section, I agreed with this argument with respect to claims 25 and 27-31 of the '660 patent, but I disagreed with respect to every other asserted claim.{2011 U.S. Dist. LEXIS 30} Accordingly, I will grant defendants' motion for summary judgment with respect claims 25 and 27-31 of the '660 patent, but I cannot grant defendants' motion on this ground with respect to the other asserted claims.

Defendants raise two more grounds for granting summary judgment with respect to direct infringement of the other asserted claims. First, defendants argue that any allegedly infringing acts under the '235, '598, '660 and '771 patents fall within the scope of a 1996 licensing agreement. Second, defendants argue that plaintiff does not have the right to sue under the '984 patent.

Finally, with respect to inducement, the question is whether plaintiff has proven inducement by defendants as a matter of law. Defendants have not moved for summary judgment on the question of inducement.

1. Direct infringement of the '235, '598, '660 and '771 patents: scope of 2006 cross license

The parties dispute whether several kinds of applications performed by the accused products sold by defendants fall within the scope of the license agreement: chimerism in the context of bone marrow transplant monitoring, cell line authentication, classifying molar specimens and determinations of fetal sex. The license extends to "any analysis, based on the measurement of the length{2011 U.S. Dist. LEXIS 31} of polynucleotide sequence containing a tandem repeat, of human genetic material for (a) use in, or preparation for, legal proceedings, or (b) analysis of biological specimens for the identification of individuals." Defendants argue that their kits fall within the scope of the license because they perform an "analysis of biological specimens for the identification of individuals."

Neither side cites much case law in favor of its position or even conducts a choice of law analysis. However, it is unnecessary to ask for supplemental briefing because it is clear from the plain language of the license and the undisputed facts that the kits in dispute do not perform an analysis "for the identification of individuals."

It is undisputed that the identity of the individual is either already known or irrelevant to the applications at issue. Plt.'s PFOF ¶ 135, dkt. #246; Dfts.' Resp. to Plt.'s PFOF ¶ 135, dkt. #257; Plt.'s PFOF ¶ 147, dkt. #246; Dfts.' Resp. to Plt.'s PFOF ¶ 147, dkt. #257; Plt.'s PFOF ¶ 150, dkt. #246; Dfts.' Resp. to Plt.'s PFOF ¶ 150, dkt. #257; Plt.'s PFOF ¶ 152, dkt. #246; Dfts.' Resp. to Plt.'s PFOF ¶ 152, dkt. #257. (Defendants dispute these proposed findings of fact on{2011 U.S. Dist. LEXIS 32} the ground that the applications involve a "human identity application," but they do not dispute the fact that the identity of the individual is already known or irrelevant in each of them.) In particular, chimerism involves determining the relative *amount* present of two different types of DNA, Plt.'s PFOF ¶ 135; classifying molar specimens involves determining whether a mole is present and what type it is; Plt.'s PFOF ¶ 147; cell line authentication involves a determination whether two cell lines are unique, Plt.'s PFOF ¶ 149. Determination of fetal sex is self-explanatory.

Defendants do not dispute plaintiff's description of these applications, but they rely on the opinion of their expert for the proposition that the applications "determine the identity, or DNA fingerprint or genetic profile of a known individual." Booker Rpt., dkt. #291-1 at ¶ 17. That is not helpful. The expert's opinion suggests that the applications may be used for the identification of particular genetic characteristics, but it does not suggest that they are used "for the identification of *individuals*." Defendants do not provide any reason to give the word "individuals" anything other than its ordinary meaning.{2011 U.S. Dist. LEXIS 33}

To the extent the parties' subjective intent is relevant, the available evidence does not support defendants' view. For example, defendants' corporate representative, Daniel Hall, testified that defendants did not have a license from plaintiff for bone marrow transplant applications, which is evidence that defendants themselves do not believe that the license covers applications in which the identity of the donor is already known. Hall Dep., dkt. #233-48, at 53-54. Defendants do not even attempt to reconcile the representative's position with their position in their summary judgment briefs that bone marrow transplant applications fall within the scope of the license. Accordingly, I am granting plaintiff's motion for summary judgment with respect to direct infringement of the asserted apparatus claims in the '235, '598, '660 and '771 patents, with the exception of claim 25 in the '660 patent and the claims that depend from claim 25.

2. Direct infringement of the '984 patent: scope of 1996 license

Defendants' argument on the '984 patent seems to be that plaintiff lacks standing to sue for infringement, though defendants do not say this explicitly. Rather, they say that plaintiff's rights under the '984 patent derive from a 1996 license that does not include{2011 U.S. Dist. LEXIS 34} the "research market" and that all of defendants' sales fall within that exception.

It is undisputed that plaintiff's rights under the '984 patent come from the 1996 license. Under that agreement, plaintiff has "an exclusive, worldwide license . . . for the HUMAN GENETIC IDENTITY and the HUMAN CLINICAL MARKET" except for "HUMAN LINKAGE ANALYSIS in the RESEARCH GENETICS FIELD OF USE." Dkt. #1-6. Defendants are simply wrong when they say that the agreement excludes the "research market" generally and they identify no reason to believe that any of their sales fall outside the human genetic identity market or the human clinical market.

Alternatively, defendants say that summary judgment is "premature" because the parties are "in the midst of arbitration proceedings" that "could result in [plaintiff] losing all rights to the ['984] patent." Dfts.' Br., dkt. #253, at 31. Defendants provide no details and they cite no authority to support this view. I decline to stay a ruling on summary judgment because of an arbitration proceeding that may or may not affect plaintiff's rights in this case at some point in the future.

Although plaintiff asserted in its opening brief that the accused products meet all of{2011 U.S. Dist. LEXIS 35} the elements of the asserted claims in the '984 patent, defendants did not challenge this assertion in their opposition brief regarding noninfringement of this patent. Accordingly, I conclude that plaintiff is entitled to summary judgment with respect to infringement of the '984 patent.

3. Inducement of the method claims

Plaintiff said little about its claim that defendants may be held liable for inducing infringement under 35 U.S.C. § 271(b). It simply summarizes the standard and then lists a number of alleged actions by defendants. It did not develop any argument in support of a view that any of these actions constitute inducement or specify which actions induce infringement of which claims. Accordingly, plaintiff has not met its burden to show that it is entitled to judgment as a matter of law on its claims under § 271(b). Because defendants did not move for summary judgment on this issue, it will proceed to trial.

C. Enablement as to the '235, '598, '660 and '771 patents

Defendants' lack of enablement argument is the flip side of its noninfringement argument, that is, if the asserted claims are not limited to the recited loci, defendants say, they are invalid because the specification does not explain how to practice any methods or kits that use loci other{2011 U.S. Dist. LEXIS 36} those recited in the claims and undue experimentation would be required to determine what other loci could be added.

Defendants' argument is not persuasive. They cite the standard that "[t]o meet the enablement requirement, the specification of a patent must teach those skilled in the art how to make and use the full scope of the claimed invention without undue experimentation." Martek Biosciences Corp. v. Nutrinova, Inc., 579 F.3d 1363, 1378 (Fed. Cir. 2009), but they misread it to mean that the "claimed invention" includes unrecited elements. Employing open-ended language does not change the invention; it is simply a way to insure that others cannot avoid infringement by adding to the invention.

If defendants were correct, nearly every open-ended claim would be invalidated. The whole point of such claims is to prevent others from avoiding infringement by adding new elements that the inventors did not anticipate at the time of the invention. If, as the court of appeals has held, patentees are entitled to draft their claims to cover unrecited elements, then it would make no sense to require patentees to explain in the specification how to practice later improvements or additions. Cf. A.B. Dick Co., 713 F.2d at 703 ("[A] pencil structurally infringing a patent claim would not become noninfringing{2011 U.S. Dist. LEXIS 37} when incorporated into a complex machine that limits or controls what the pencil can write. *Neither would infringement be negated simply because the patentee failed to contemplate use of the pencil in that environment.*") (Emphasis added).

Defendants cite two cases to support their argument, but neither of them addresses the question whether a patentee must enable unrecited elements. Rather, both of them involved an applicant that used a broad term in the claim and then failed to explain how to practice the invention with respect to particular aspects of that term. In re Vaeck, 947 F.2d 488, 495 (Fed. Cir. 1991) (affirming patent office's conclusion that claim was not enabled because applicant included "cyanobacteria" element without explaining in specification which cyanobacteria could be used); Sitrick v. Dreamworks, LLC, 516 F.3d 993, 1000 (Fed. Cir. 2008) (claim that disclosed invention related to both movies and video games not enabled because specification did not teach how to practice invention with movies). In the absence of case law requiring the patentee to enable his invention with respect to unrecited elements, I decline to impose such a requirement.

D. Obviousness as to the '235, '598, '660 and '771 patents

The parties agree that all elements of the claims were known in the prior art, with the exception{2011 U.S. Dist. LEXIS 38} of the particular combinations of loci to be co-amplified. Under 35 U.S.C. § 103(a), a claim is invalid "if the differences between the claimed subject matter and the prior art are such that the subject matter as a whole would have been obvious at the time the invention was made to a person having ordinary skill in the art to which said subject matter pertains." Star Scientific, Inc. v. R.J. Reynolds Tobacco Co., 655 F.3d 1364, 1374 (Fed. Cir. 2011) (internal quotations and alterations omitted). Defendants have the burden to show by clear and convincing evidence that the asserted claims are obvious. Hybritech Inc. v. Monoclonal Antibodies, Inc., 802 F.2d 1367, 1375 (Fed. Cir.1986).

Defendants advance two theories of obviousness. The first is the only theory included in defendants' expert report. It is contingent on defendants' argument that the claims are not enabled unless the specification shows how to practice the inventions using loci not recited in the claims:

> In the event that the Promega patents are actually deemed [to] teach and enable skilled artisans to multiplex sets of loci other than those listed in the claims, i.e., arbitrary sets of loci, then the claims would have been obvious in light of the prior art because the prior art would have already taught and enabled the same. Sun Decl., Ex. 8 (Struhl Invalidity Report) ¶ 45. In other words, if trial and error{2011 U.S. Dist. LEXIS 39} as disclosed in the Promega patents constitutes an enabling disclosure for multiplexing arbitrary sets of loci, then the prior art, which already taught trial and error, would also already have taught multiplexing of arbitrary sets of loci.Dfts.' Br., dkt. #245, at 44. Because I have rejected defendants' enablement theory, this argument is moot.

Defendants' second theory is that the new loci combinations are not a "significant" difference from the prior art because "the selection of the number of loci and the specific loci for use in a multiplex is merely an arbitrary choice." Id. at 45-56. This argument suffers from multiple problems. To begin with, it seems to be an afterthought because defendants' expert does not discuss it and defendants have submitted no proposed findings of fact about it. As I noted in the introduction, the court will not consider facts if they are included in a brief but not in the party's proposed findings of fact. Defendants cite United States v. Murphy Oil USA, Inc., 143 F. Supp. 2d 1054, 1064 (W.D. Wis. 2001), for the proposition that parties should not include legal conclusions in their proposed findings of fact. That is obviously correct, but unhelpful. Expert opinions and descriptions of the prior art are not legal conclusions. In any event,{2011 U.S. Dist. LEXIS 40} even if I considered the allegations in defendants' brief, defendants cite no evidence showing that it would be obvious to a person of ordinary skill in the art that combinations of loci in the claims can be successfully co-amplified. Because defendants bear the burden of persuasion with respect to invalidity, plaintiff's motion for summary judgment must be granted on the issue of obviousness.

E. Willful Infringement

Finally, plaintiff has moved for summary judgment on the question of willfulness, which it bears the burden to prove by clear and convincing evidence. nCube Corp. v. Seachange Intern., Inc., 436 F.3d 1317, 1319 (Fed. Cir. 2006). Plaintiff has not shown that it is entitled to judgment as a matter of law on this issue. "'[W]illful' action is quintessentially a question of fact, for it depends on findings of culpable intent and deliberate or negligent wrongdoing." Biotec Biologische Naturverpackungen GmbH & Co. KG v. Biocorp, Inc., 249 F.3d 1341, 1356 (Fed. Cir. 2001). In fact, plaintiff cites no cases in which a court concluded that the plaintiff was entitled to summary judgment on willfulness. Perhaps more important, plaintiff's argument on willfulness is undeveloped, making up a page of their opening brief and consisting of little more than a few quotations from documents prepared by one employee of defendants. This is insufficient to show as a matter{2011 U.S. Dist. LEXIS 41} of law that plaintiff is entitled to a finding of willfulness.

ORDER

IT IS ORDERED that

1. The motion for partial summary judgment filed by defendants Life Technologies Corporation, Invitrogen IP Holdings, Inc. and Applied Biosystems, LLC, dkt. #234, is GRANTED with respect to plaintiff Promega Corporation's claim of infringement of claims 25 and 27-31 of U.S. Patent No. 5,843,660 and defendants' counterclaims for noninfringement of the same claims. Plaintiff's complaint is DISMISSED as to those claims. Defendants' motion is DENIED in all other respects.

2. Plaintiff's motion for summary judgment, dkt. #227, is GRANTED with respect to the following claims of infringement:

> AmpFISTR COfiler PCR Ampliflication Kit infringes claims 23 and 27 of U.S. Patent No.6,221,598 and claim 42 of U.S. Patent No. Re 37,984;
>
> AmpFISTR Profiler PCR Amplification Kit infringes claims 10, 23-24, 27 and 33 of the '598 patent and claim 42 of the '984 patent;
>
> AmpFISTR Identifiler PCR Amplification Kit infringes claims 10, 23-24 and 27 of the '598 patent, claims 18-19 and 21-23 of U.S. Patent No. 6,479,235, claim 5 of U.S. Patent No. 7,008,771 and claim 42 of the '984 patent;
>
> AmpFISTR Profiler Plus PCR Amplification Kit infringes claim 42 of the '984 patent; and
>
> AmpFISTR Yfiler PCR Amplification Kit infringes claim 42 of the '984 patent.The motion is DENIED as to all other claims of infringement{2011 U.S. Dist. LEXIS 42} and inducing infringement.

2. Plaintiff's motion for summary judgment, dkt. #227, is GRANTED with respect to defendants' affirmative defenses and counterclaims that the '235, '598, '660 and '771 patents are invalid because they are anticipated, obvious or not enabled. Plaintiff's motion is DENIED with respect to its claim of willfulness.

3. Plaintiff's motion to disregard facts not included in the proposed findings of fact, dkt. #262, is GRANTED. Plaintiff's motion for leave to file a reply brief in support of that motion, dkt. #293, is DENIED as unnecessary.

Entered this 29th day of November, 2011.

BY THE COURT:

/s/ BARBARA B. CRABB

District Judge

## Author Bio

The author apologizes to the reader for some redundancy, caused by physical limitations in writing by hand one-cogent paper containing all facts. This book is the product of many years of research and is meant to help those wrongfully accused and or convicted.
~F. Finch

www.ingramcontent.com/pod-product-compliance
Lightning Source LLC
Chambersburg PA
CBHW081406070526
44583CB00020B/2702